# ROUTLEDGE LIBRARY EDITIONS: LIBRARY AND INFORMATION SCIENCE

Volume 26

# DECLINING ACQUISITIONS BUDGETS

# DECLINING ACQUISITIONS BUDGETS
Allocation, Collection Development and Impact Communication

Edited by
SUL H. LEE

LONDON AND NEW YORK

First published in 1993 by The Haworth Press, Inc.

This edition first published in 2020
by Routledge
2 Park Square, Milton Park, Abingdon, Oxon OX14 4RN

and by Routledge
52 Vanderbilt Avenue, New York, NY 10017

*Routledge is an imprint of the Taylor & Francis Group, an informa business*

© 1993 The Haworth Press, Inc.

All rights reserved. No part of this book may be reprinted or reproduced or utilised in any form or by any electronic, mechanical, or other means, now known or hereafter invented, including photocopying and recording, or in any information storage or retrieval system, without permission in writing from the publishers.

*Trademark notice*: Product or corporate names may be trademarks or registered trademarks, and are used only for identification and explanation without intent to infringe.

*British Library Cataloguing in Publication Data*
A catalogue record for this book is available from the British Library

ISBN: 978-0-367-34616-4 (Set)
ISBN: 978-0-429-34352-0 (Set) (ebk)
ISBN: 978-0-367-41044-5 (Volume 26) (hbk)
ISBN: 978-0-367-41047-6 (Volume 26) (pbk)
ISBN: 978-0-367-81443-4 (Volume 26) (ebk)

**Publisher's Note**
The publisher has gone to great lengths to ensure the quality of this reprint but points out that some imperfections in the original copies may be apparent.

**Disclaimer**
The publisher has made every effort to trace copyright holders and would welcome correspondence from those they have been unable to trace.

# Declining Acquisitions Budgets: Allocation, Collection Development and Impact Communication

Sul H. Lee
Editor

The Haworth Press, Inc.
New York • London • Norwood (Australia)

*Declining Acquisitions Budgets: Allocation, Collection Development and Impact Communication* has also been published as *Journal of Library Administration,* Volume 19, Number 2 1993.

© 1993 by The Haworth Press, Inc. All rights reserved. No part of this work may be reproduced or utilized in any form or by any means, electronic or mechanical, including photocopying, microfilm and recording, or by any information storage and retrieval system, without permission in writing from the publisher. Printed in the United States of America.

The development, preparation, and publication of this work has been undertaken with great care. However, the publisher, employees, editors, and agents of The Haworth Press and all imprints of The Haworth Press, Inc., including The Haworth Medical Press and Pharmaceutical Products Press, are not responsible for any errors contained herein or for consequences that may ensue from use of materials or information contained in this work. Opinions expressed by the author(s) are not necessarily those of The Haworth Press, Inc.

The Haworth Press, Inc., 10 Alice Street, Binghamton, NY 13904-1580 USA

**Library of Congress Cataloging-in-Publication Data**

Declining acquisitions budgets: allocation, collection development and impact communication/Sul H. Lee, editor.
    p. cm.
    "Also published as Journal of library administration, volume 19, number 2, 1993"-T.p. verso.
    Includes bibliographical references.
    ISBN 1-56024-613-8 (acid-free paper).-ISBN 1-56024-614-6 (pkb.: acid-free paper)
    1. Collection development (Libraries)-United States-Congresses. 2. Library materials budgets-United States-Congresses. I. Lee, Sul H.
Z687.2.U6D43   1993
025.2' 187073-dc20                                                   93-39258
                                                                                                 CIP

# Declining Acquisitions Budgets: Allocation, Collection Development and Impact Communication

## CONTENTS

| | |
|---|---|
| Introduction<br>    *Sul H. Lee* | 1 |
| The Director's Role in the Acquisitions Dilemma<br>    *Nancy L. Eaton* | 3 |
| Is It Possible to Develop Libraries Without Resources?<br>    *Leonard Schrift* | 19 |
| Crisis and Opportunity: Reevaluating Acquisitions Budgeting in an Age of Transition<br>    *Ross Atkinson* | 33 |
| Allocating Library Acquisitions Budgets in an Era of Declining or Static Funding<br>    *Judy Webster* | 57 |
| Justifying Collection Budgets: Indexing Materials Costs<br>    *Gay N. Dannelly* | 75 |
| Access vs. Ownership: What Is Most Cost Effective in the Sciences<br>    *Anthony W. Ferguson*<br>    *Kathleen Kehoe* | 89 |

Toward a Calculus of Collection Development 101
*Charles Hamaker*

The Role of the Serials Vendor in the Collection Assessment
and Evaluation Process 125
*Kathleen Born*

# Introduction

Libraries throughout the country have been faced with the rising costs of information for over a decade. Now, reductions in library budgets are adding to the dilemma. In response to the concerns associated with these issues the University of Oklahoma Libraries in association with the OU Foundation held a conference in Oklahoma City on February 25 and 26, 1992 entitled, "Declining Acquisitions Budgets: Allocation, Collection Development, and Communication of Impact." The papers delivered at the conference are presented in this volume and will also be available as a special monograph.

Throughout the program, the conference speakers provided thought-provoking presentations which touched on library, business, and societal issues. Nancy Eaton, Dean of Library Services at Iowa State University, explored the many roles of a library director in communicating issues and developing strategies in response to economic and technological change. Leonard Schrift, President and CEO of Ballen Booksellers International, highlighted issues relating to the publishing industry and discussed, among other ideas, a formula for maintaining book collections.

The next group of presentations focused upon acquisitions assumptions and practices. Ross Atkinson, Assistant University Librarian for Collection Development and Preservation at Cornell University suggests the purposes for acquisitions budgets must be questioned and new strategies developed. Judy Webster, Head, Acquisitions and Processing Team at the University of Tennessee, continues the examination of acquisitions budgets through a review of traditional theories and strategies for allocating acquisitions budgets. She proposes that tradition needs to be altered in favor of more flexible and informed budgeting. Gay Dannelly, Collection Development Officer at Ohio State University presents an example of new practices in acquisitions budgeting through a discussion of the Ohio State University libraries indexing system.

Anthony Ferguson, Associate University Librarian at Columbia University, and Kathleen Kehoe, Reference/Collection Development Librarian in the Science and Engineering Division at Columbia University, provide a discussion on the changing emphasis from ownership to access in collection development through a study completed at Columbia University's Science Library. Charles Hamaker, Assistant Dean for Collection Development at Louisiana State University, reviews the issues surrounding the rising costs of published materials, the increase in published information, and the question of ownership of information. He then proceeds to outline a project to gather circulation information for use in collection development.

Kathleen Born, Director of the Academic Division of EBSCO Subscription Services, completes the papers with a discussion of the services a subscription vendor can offer librarians working on collection development and acquisitions.

As in past conferences, the papers created interesting discussion which cannot be recorded in this publication. It is hoped the publication of the papers will provide the reader with insight into these important issues and also create additional discussion of them.

I would like to thank Wilbur Stolt, who provided editorial assistance for this volume, Don Hudson, who served as conference coordinator, and Linda Roman, who assisted with the secretarial duties. Their help is greatly appreciated.

*Sul H. Lee*

# The Director's Role in the Acquisitions Dilemma

Nancy L. Eaton

## INTRODUCTION

For much too long the crisis in scholarly publishing has been viewed by senior public and university administrators as the "library's budget problem." In large part that was our own doing. Year after year we made special budget requests based upon more than normal inflation in the publishing industry. Only when the national, state, and local economies could no longer support such unprecedented increases did we begin to examine the underlying causes of these unrelenting price increases and to look at systemic causes outside the library.

As the publishing industry has received more critical scrutiny, it has become more common to describe the economic plight of libraries not as a "library problem" but rather as a national problem for the educational and research communities. Viewed in that light, many people and organizations must play a role in reconceptualizing the scholarly communication process while also trying to maintain critical components of the current system as that process takes place. This paper explores the specific role of the library's dean or

Nancy L. Eaton is Dean of Library Services, Iowa State University of Science and Technology, Ames, IA.

[Haworth co-indexing entry note]: "The Director's Role in the Acquisitions Dilemma." Eaton, Nancy L. Co-published simultaneously in *Journal of Library Administration* (The Haworth Press, Inc.) Vol. 19, No. 2, 1993, pp. 3-18: and: *Declining Acquisitions Budgets: Allocation, Collection Development and Impact Communication* (ed: Sul H. Lee) The Haworth Press, Inc., 1993, pp. 3-18. Multiple copies of this article/chapter may be purchased from The Haworth Document Delivery Center [1-800-3-HAWORTH; 9:00 a.m. - 5:00 p.m. (EST)].

© 1993 by The Haworth Press, Inc. All rights reserved.

director in that process. For the sake of simplicity, the term "director" will refer to both titles.

## THE DIRECTOR'S ROLE

### Symbolism

While library staff will be more immersed in the details of the selection, acquisition, and management of collections, it is the director who must represent those issues to the broader community. Given the magnitude and complexity of the changes before us, we need to think of this as a political process, not a budgetary process. We know how important symbolism can be in the political process; and a key tool for that process is public relations. The library director should take symbolism very seriously. His/her role is first and foremost a public relations role to articulate the issues, to build coalitions, to focus resources on the problem, and to pressure for change.

### Catalyst for Change

Because this is a political process, there are many constituencies and viewpoints to be facilitated: funding agencies, university administrators, faculty and researchers, students, the library staff, consortia partners, and (increasingly) external clientele. And there are the suppliers of information to be factored in: authors, publishers, government agencies, vendors, telecommunications and computing professionals. It is increasingly important that the director be willing to conceptualize this change process in language understandable outside the library profession, to project time frames for the process, to break the process down by constituency interests, and to "hit the road" to mediate and facilitate the process.

Pleading for more money to match inflation and the fluctuations in the dollar is no longer viable unless it is also accompanied by new strategies that hold promise for changing the system. Our presidents, provosts, and politicians have heard our message and basically understand the dilemma. They now want us to pursue strategies for changing the current situation. Most of them understand that this requires risk-taking and that there are no clear solutions. At a minimum they want to be presented with some new approaches that they can invest in if they are also going to continue to have to shore up the current system in the near-term. For example, on November 13, 1990, the Executive Committee of the National Association of State Universities and Land-Grant Colleges (NASULGC) passed a resolution drafted by its Library Committee in support of ARL serials reports and recommendations. These ARL recommendations advocated consumer actions, encouragement of greater competition to the commercial sector, and partnerships with scholarly groups to address the information "crisis." The NASULGC Executive Committee consists of presidents and representatives from each of the NASULGC Divisions and is the organization's policy-making group.[1]

*Accountability*

Beyond the frustration of presidents, provosts, and funding agencies with the annual plea for more than normal inflation, there is the reality that higher education in general is in financial crisis and that all academic administrators are being held to a higher measure of accountability than in the past. Therefore, in addition to trying to understand the dynamics and economics of the publishing world, library directors must also question how well we are using the resources we have. The old 20/80 rule of thumb—20 percent of our collections meet 80 percent of demand—is no longer credible to our senior administrators and funding agencies, given the fiscal climate.

Directors must encourage the development of more refined methods of matching user needs with strategies for supplying that material in more efficient ways. Unfortunately the research process and our open stack libraries do not lend themselves to easy analysis. Even basic data-gathering is difficult. Much of the data we do collect has little to do with user needs. We will have to do better in the future. Developing such analytical methods, gathering meaningful data, and analyzing user behavior patterns will take time. However, to have such efforts visible will help facilitate our interim budget requests.

### Establishing Strategies and Identifying Allies

The collective challenge of library directors is to work toward strategies that different constituencies can invest in, to find allies to help promote those strategies, and to move those strategies into every possible arena–professional association meetings, governmental debates, strategic plans, budget processes, funded projects, etc. Directors must be opportunistic to move this agenda forward. A variety of strategies and alliances have been mobilized to date.

*Association for Research Libraries.* ARL has become a key component of ARL directors' strategies. The Office of Scientific and Academic Publishing headed by Ann Okerson was established in 1989 at the request of ARL directors who felt that publishing prices had to be attacked as a national problem, that it could not be successfully confronted at the local level only, and that expertise and better analysis of the problem needed to be focused on the issues. "The new office is designed to identify and influence the forces affecting the production, dissemination, and use of scientific and scholarly information."[2] The data now being provided by that office is extremely useful in documenting such things as publisher behavior, library expenditures, and changes in journal costs. The office was funded by a dues increase voted by the ARL directors, which indicates the power of collective action.

*Scholarly and Academic Associations.* On behalf of ARL directors, ARL has begun to forge alliances with other scholarly and governmental bodies to expand this collective action, including the American Council of Learned Societies, NASULGC, the Association of American University Presses, the Consortium of Social Science Associations, EDUCOM, CAUSE, the Association of American Universities, American Association for the Advancement of Science, and the American Academy of Arts and Sciences.[3] According to Duane E. Webster, ARL Executive Director, "These strategic alliances are increasingly the best means available to the Association to influence the future. The success of recent and ongoing ARL initiatives underscores the importance of continuing to invest in developing these alliances."[4] ARL initiatives draw heavily upon its members, the ARL directors, to participate in these activities. In addition, many directors have become personally active in

NASULGC, EDUCOM, and CAUSE as a means of influencing their agendas concerning scholarly and electronic publishing.

*Library Consortia.* Most academic libraries belong to regional or state consortia such as the Big-Ten Consortium for Inter-institutional Cooperation (CIC) or the Association of Big-Eight Universities (ABEU). These groups can be used to leverage access to presidents and provosts and to bring consortia resources to bear on testing new strategies. For instance, the CIC is investigating the possibility of mounting databases through the CIC on behalf of all its libraries and to take responsibility for archiving selected electronic publications. The library directors of ABEU have been consolidating regional information about serial cancellations and have presented this information to their provosts to underscore the aggregate loss of access to periodicals regionally.

*Special Initiatives or Projects.* Increasingly library directors have been committing library resources to joint projects with other constituency groups in order that new approaches to scholarly publishing be investigated jointly among the key players. For instance, the Cornell University Agricultural Library has an initiative on electronic publishing in partnership with OCLC, Chemical Abstracts, and Bellcore. Iowa State University has signed several cooperative agreements with the National Agricultural Library to pursue electronic distribution of information and cooperative collection development in the area of biotechnology. Virginia Polytechnic Institute (VPI) has a major initiative called the "Electronic Village." The Red Sage Experiment is a collaboration among the University of California-San Francisco, Springer Verlag, and AT&T to experiment with 47 biomedical journals in electronic format.[5] The TULIP Project between Elsevier and a selected group of research universities has those institutions mounting full text of Elsevier journals under various search engines and making them available over campus networks. These projects have, by and large, been initiated by library directors in collaboration with other administrators in their institutions. In many cases, these projects add significant workloads and stress to local library staffs. Clearly, the direction and priority is set by the library director as part of a larger agenda for the library and the campus. It is extremely important that the reasons for committing staff time and library resources to these projects be articulated in a persuasive manner to faculty and library staff.

## Educating the Faculty, Students, and Alumni

Because library directors have had to plead their case for funding each year, they have spent considerable time and effort in educating those administrators above them in the intricacies of the acquisitions "dilemma." Faculty, on the other hand, usually become aware of the issues when the library announces a serials cancellation project or when they request that the library purchase a new title and are refused. They vaguely understand that inflation for library materials is higher than normal inflation; and they have heard a lot of half-truths about how electronic publishing will solve all the library's problems. Very few faculty are informed about the economics of publishing within their own discipline, however. They are interested in having access to the publications they need to teach and conduct their own research, and they want to publish the results of their own research as part of the distribution of knowledge and the academic reward system. Until recently, most faculty viewed the library's budget problems as something to be taken care of by the central administration, period!

In 1991, the director of the Iowa State University Library and the Vice Provost for Research jointly sponsored a seminar for selected ISU faculty who either edited scholarly journals or who were on the editorial boards of such journals. The intent of the seminar was to expose this selected group of about fifty influential faculty members to background information on the current economic issues of scholarly publishing and then to test on them the viability of a number of strategies being proposed within various national groups. Most of those in attendance found the information provided to be new information that they were unaware of. Even more interesting was the fact that most of them felt quite helpless to influence their publishers' behavior, though they were more optimistic about being able to influence the editorial boards or committees of their own professional associations. Several editors said that they had asked for pricing information from their publishers and were refused. They asked that the library begin to supply them with pricing information within their disciplines in order that they could better understand and influence scholarly publishing within their own areas of expertise.

This particular experience illustrates the huge educational process we face with faculty if they are to understand why libraries are moving toward a model of "access to information" rather than local ownership, or why libraries are being so aggressive about electronic information as a necessary component of scholarly publishing in the future. We must do a better job of informing faculty if we expect them to support these new directions. And the information must be packaged discipline by discipline for faculty to understand it, relate to it, or want to try to influence it. The library staff also needs to view the information discipline by discipline, since there are different dynamics and problems in different disciplines.

The resources necessary to mount an educational process of the magnitude needed to do discipline by discipline analysis of publishing and pricing patterns is significant. Some of this information is now being provided by the ARL Office of Scientific and Academic Publishing. Table 1 is an example of the kind of data now being made available for use by ARL directors and library staff.[6]

To the extent that we can gather this kind of data in a collaborative way, we will save time and energy. But much of the analysis that is campus-specific or in disciplines not yet addressed by ARL will require resources of library collection development and acquisitions staff. The library director will have to make this a priority, assign resources to accomplish it, and utilize this data in strategic presentations to faculty, administrators, and alumni as part of his/her public relations role. This data can be powerful in faculty discussions, in budget presentations, and in fundraising efforts. An example is the leadership role that Donald W. Koepp, University Librarian at Princeton University, took against unprecedented price increases by Pergamon Press in 1992. Mr. Koepp led a campus discussion about these dramatic price increases that resulted in Princeton University faculty agreeing that the library would cancel sufficient Pergamon journals so that the total cost to Princeton in 1992 would be no more than the cost in 1991 plus the percentage of inflationary increase in the allocations for each department; this resulted in the cancellation of almost one-fourth of their Pergamon subscriptions. Table 2 indicates cost data put together by library staff on Pergamon prices.[7]

Students, by and large, are interested in how periodical cuts will

# TABLE 1

## AMONG THE LEADING MASS SPECTROMETRY JOURNALS

OSAP is continuing to highlight journals in a variety of disciplines. We are asking distinguished faculty members on ARL campuses to identify the leading journals in their research areas. Our second effort was in the field of mass spectrometry, where the researcher identified 6 of his most heavily consulted titles. Data is supplied from ARL science library collections and records. All prices given are for subscriptions for the 1991 year and were verified by the publisher.

| Title | Publisher | Volume | Number of issues | Pages | Price (for 1991) | Price per page |
|---|---|---|---|---|---|---|
| Biological Mass Spectrometry (1974+)[1] | Wiley (Chicester) | 20 (1991) | 12 | 824 | $1195 | $1.45 per page |
| International Journal of Mass Spectrometry and Ion Processes (1968+) | Elsevier (Amsterdam) | 103(2)–111 (1991) | varies[2] | 2974 | $1376.35[3] | $.46 per page |
| JASMS (Journal of the American Society of Mass Spectrometry) (1990+) | Elsevier (NY) | 2 (1991) | 6 | 522 | $250[4] | $.48 per page |
| Mass Spectrometry Reviews (1982+) | Wiley (NY) | 10 (1991) | 6 | 670 | $280 | $.42 per page |
| Organic Mass Spectrometry (1968+) | Wiley (Chicester) | 26 (1991) | 12 | 1,136 | $975 | $.86 per page |
| Rapid Communications in Mass Spectrometry (1987+) | Wiley (Chicester) | 5 (1991) | 12 | 240 | $545 | $2.27 per page |

[1] Continues Biomedical & Environmental Mass Spectrometry.
[2] Some confusion is possible. Volume 103 had two issues, n. 1 dated Dec. 31, 1990 and n. 2 dated January 1, 1991.
[3] This price calculated at a .5832 October 1990 conversion rate and disregards a $240 postage fee.
[4] Free to society members.

## TABLE 2

### EXAMPLES OF PERGAMON
### PRICE INCREASES TO PRINCETON

Pergamon Press publishes over 400 serials. According to Princeton staff, on Pergamon's September 1 invoice to Princeton for 1992 journal subscriptions, the average increase was approximately 30%. The following titles are those that increased in price by over 50%. Where the invoice bills for two years, the price below represents 1/2 of the renewal price. Prices are in U.S. dollars.

| Title | 1991 | 1992 | Increase |
|---|---|---|---|
| International journal of solids & structures | 584.25 | 1,572.25 | 169% |
| Solid-state electronics | 460.75 | 1,049.75 | 128% |
| Rheology abstracts | 142.50 | 304.00 | 113% |
| Carbon | 375.25 | 745.75 | 99% |
| Organic geochemistry | 560.00 | 1,050.00 | 88% |
| Electrochimica acta | 688.75 | 1,239.75 | 80% |
| International journal of non-linear mechanics | 327.75 | 560.50 | 71% |
| Molecular immunology | 532.00 | 912.00 | 71% |
| International journal of heat & mass transfer | 817.00 | 1,377.50 | 69% |
| Automatica | 356.25 | 593.75 | 67% |
| Journal of the mechanics & physics of solids | 545.00 | 910.00 | 67% |
| Journal of psychosomatic research | 270.75 | 427.50 | 58% |
| Tetrahedron | 2,740.75 | 4,332.00 | 58% |
| International journal of multiphase flow | 380.00 | 593.75 | 56% |
| Journal of aerosol science | 403.75 | 631.75 | 56% |
| Vision research | 570.00 | 888.25 | 56% |
| Personality and ind. differences | 300.00 | 465.00 | 55% |
| Polyhedron | 1,111.50 | 1,710.00 | 54% |
| Vacuum | 389.50 | 598.50 | 54% |
| Water research | 707.75 | 1,087.75 | 54% |
| Developmental & comparative immunology | 305.00 | 465.00 | 53% |
| European polymer journal | 650.75 | 997.50 | 53% |
| Deep sea research w/oceanographic literature review | 935.75 | 1,415.50 | 51% |
| Physics of metals & metallography | 821.75 | 1,244.50 | 51% |
| Tetrahedron letters | 2,579.25 | 3,885.50 | 51% |

affect their ability to do their assignments. Here the library director may find himself/herself caught between the demand by students to protect undergraduate resources and the demands of faculty for expensive research materials. This type of priority setting should emanate from campus deliberations on university priorities; and the library director should be part of those deliberations. With the new national emphasis on improving the quality of undergraduate education, it is now easier to protect those resources against the insatiable demand for more research materials; but that has not always been the case.

The other major audiences needing education are donors and alumni. Increasingly library directors are expected to do fundraising to help supplement the library acquisitions budget through collection endowments. Particularly at state institutions, alumni and donors may question why they should give to the library, since it is funded by the legislature. These individuals have to be made aware of the trends in costs for providing library materials if they are to be persuaded to make a contribution to the library. It is usually the library director who is responsible for this kind of communication, either one-on-one, at alumni gatherings, or via articles in alumni or development publications.

## *AUDIENCES*

The director's leadership role in dealing with the acquisitions dilemma requires that he/she be aware of the audience that is the target for action, since that will determine the approach to be used. These audiences include the university administration, computing staff, faculty, students, alumni and donors, external clientele that want services, consortia partners, vendors or publishers who supply publications and who may be collaborators on projects, and library staff. Each of these audiences looks at the problem(s) from a particular point of view. Strategies and information should be adapted to address the particular concerns of each audience. While directors do this informally, a more formal approach has benefits. A "strategy checklist" by typeof audience illustrates the thinking process that should take place (see Audience Strategy Checklist).

Let us take two typical target audiences and play out the scenar-

## AUDIENCE STRATEGY CHECKLIST

Audience:

Interest/point of view of audie

Objective/outcome sought:

Symbolism:

Data needed:

Allies:

Short-term strategies:

Long-term strategies:

Public relations plan:

Resources needed:

## AUDIENCE STRATEGY CHECKLIST
### Example 1

Audience:   President
            Provost

Interest/point of view of audience:

(1) Request for annual budget increase for library materials and access;

(2) How library expenditures map to campus and college strategic plans;

(3) How library is reallocating internally to support changes in library and campus priorities;

(4) Strategies to follow as a university to support national efforts to change the system of scholarly publishing;

(5) If the president has one-time end-of-year funds, how can we use them to best leverage #1-4.

Objective/outcome sought:

(1) Integrate library strategies with university strategies, so that this is not viewed as an annual library budget problem.
(2) Show that the library is already addressing some of these problems through its own strategic plan and reallocation.
(3) Identify projects or investments that the president and provost are willing to support financially.

Symbolism:

(1) Show library as progressive; director as a leader.
(2) Stress library as "heart of the university."
(3) Meet the goals of the president and provost. (Hidden agenda: raise visibility of the university and enhance its national stature.)

Data needed:

(1) ARL trend data on budget increases, decreases in library purchases of serials and monographs, increases in ILL.
(2) Plot university library data against ARL data to show how it fares by comparison.
(3) ARL data by discipline to show variation in page costs by publisher and inflation by publisher and discipline.
(4) Data on ABEU library serial cancellations.
(5) Draw conclusions from trend lines that support need for "access" model; show "access" strategies.

Allies:

ARL
University Library Committee
Collection Development Department
Director of the Computation Center &
 Telecommunications Office.
ABEU library directors

Short-term strategies:

(1) Encourage president and provost to discuss this issue as a national problem at NASULGC and AAU meetings. Prepare this university to take positions as national strategies evolve.

(2) Have short list of how end-of-year money could be used.

(3) Have provost and vice-provost for research support library's explanations to faculty by joint discussions with dean's council, with President's Council, and with faculty.

(4) Present annual budget information in the context of university, college, and library strategic plans, so that there is confidence that funds are being used wisely.

Long-term strategies:

(1) Try to have president and provost address promotion and tenure reward system as part of what is driving the "publish or perish" syndrome; get them to open a campus dialogue about alternative reward systems.

(2) Have provost and deans consider how electronic publications will be evaluated for promotion and tenure.

(3) Continue to build infrastructure on campus and nationally that can support electronic publishing and document delivery.

(4) Compete for grants or private funds to mount pilot projects with networking and electronic information to gain local experience and to be seen as a "player."

Public relations plan:

(1) Private two hour briefing for president and provost.

(2) Periodic briefings for college deans and Library Committee.

(3) Director becomes visible on several national components of the publishing debate, either as PI for a funded project, by writing white paper(s) for a national organization, or by publishing articles in prominent journals.

(4) Inform library staff of strategy and outcomes and seek their council on each component.

(5) Cultivate good working relationships with computing and telecommunications directors so that they are willing to partner on projects.

Resources needed:

(1) Director allocate personal time to prepare for private briefing. BE PREPARED!

(2) Library and consortia staff to compile data.

(3) Identify staff and time to write grant(s) or proposal(s).

---

## AUDIENCE STRATEGY CHECKLIST
### Example 2

---

Audience: Chemistry Department faculty

Interest/point of view of audience: Access to journal literature

Objective/outcome sought: (1) New strategy on cancellation of print journals; and (2) Willingness to experiment with "access" model.

Symbolism: Show leadership, connect appropriate staff to project.

Data needed: (1) Cost analysis for journals in discipline; (2) ARL trendline data; and (3) Better use statistics.

Allies: (1) Library Committee; (2) Senior faculty members; (3) Department chair; and (4) Faculty who edit journals or who are on editorial boards in the discipline.

Short-term strategies: (1) Try to get faculty support for Princeton approach to specific publishers whose prices are increasing out of proportion to costs; and (2) Refine method for deciding what to cancel and what to add.

Long-term strategies: (1) Work nationally and locally to improve ILL/document delivery systems to reduce time lags between request and delivery and to deliver articles to the office or desktop; (2) Refine methods for measuring use and demand; and

Public relations plan: (1) Use client-driven approach, e.g., show interest in their needs; (2) Use this as opportunity to educate and build support base; and (3) Look for opportunities to work with journal editors or editorial boards in professional associations in discipline-specific publishing ventures.

Resources needed: (1) Eight hours of director's time with department and library staff; (2) Collection Development staff time to compile data and work with department faculty (estimated two bibliographers at 40 hours each); and (3) Encourage faculty to work through their professional associations.

---

ios for each: In example 1 the president and provost of the university, since they determine budgetary resources for the library each year; and in example 2 the chemistry department faculty of a major research university.

## *CONCLUSION*

We usually think of acquisitions as a function within the library that is handled by technical services and collection development staff. However, as we grapple with the larger systemic issues of scholarly publishing and try to influence that system, the library director or dean has a visible role to play with a broad spectrum of individuals and organizations that influence the system of scholarly publishing. In addition, the director must retain the confidence of his/her campus constituency by convincing them that he/she is providing appropriate leadership that will eventually help change the system and make it more economically sound.

In the short-term, university administrators and funding agencies are more likely to continue to fund the current system if they believe that the library administration is reallocating internally to do its share to meet the annual financial need before automatically asking for inflation increases. In order to shift resources internally, the library will need better data on use of materials and on patron needs.

This will require that we improve our analytical capabilities, including library staff expertise to do more surveys and quantitative analysis and including the ability to capture data from our automated systems. Directors must recognize this as a library priority and be willing to make resource commitments accordingly.

## NOTES

1. Okerson, Ann. "NASULGC Resolution Supports ARL Serials Initiatives." *ARL: A Bimonthly Newsletter of Research Library Issues and Actions* 154 (January 4, 1991):8.

2. "Membership Votes to Fund Office of Scientific and Academic Publishing," *ARL Newsletter* 148:2.

3. See articles in *ARL: A Bimonthly Newsletter of Research Library Issues and Actions* 159:2 and 160:12-13.

4. *ARL: A Bimonthly Newsletter of Research Library Issues and Actions* 159:3.

5. Reported by Czeslaw Jan Grycz, University of California Office of the President, at a presentation to the OCLC Users Council, Columbus, Ohio, February 8, 1993.

6. *ARL: A Bimonthly Newsletter of Research Library Issues and Actions* 162:11.

7. *ARL: A Bimonthly Newsletter of Research Library Issues and Actions* 160:1-2.

# Is It Possible to Develop Libraries Without Resources?

## Leonard Schrift

Over the course of the last ten years, this conference has addressed an almost infinite number of topics and aspects concerning the issue of acquisitions budgets and its effect on library collections. I have attended most meetings, and from time to time have been invited to speak on these very same issues.

What has evolved in my own eyes, is not so much as a clear picture of the issues and problems, but perhaps a larger view of the matrix, and particularly the spectrum of the current dilemma and its future.

The issues and their potential solution go far beyond the library, beyond the university, much beyond the state, and perhaps even beyond the federal government. The issues and their various aspects and form are global, and in all likelihood will lead to a multitude of separate and definitive solutions worldwide.

If anyone in the library world would try to base either the long-term planning process or the shorter-term decision making action on the tenets of classical marketing and economic theory, we all are doomed to the rude awakening of a ringing failure. At present, there is precious little in both the universe of academic publishers and libraries to resemble the large number of buyers and sellers whose rational, independent response to the laws of supply and demand result in the "logical" functioning of the marketplace.

---

Leonard Schrift is President and CEO of Ballen Booksellers International, Inc., Hauppauge, NY.

[Haworth co-indexing entry note]: "Is It Possible to Develop Libraries Without Resources?" Schrift, Leonard. Co-published simultaneously in *Journal of Library Administration* (The Haworth Press, Inc.) Vol. 19, No. 2, 1993, pp. 19-32: and: *Declining Acquisitions Budgets: Allocation, Collection Development and Impact Communication* (ed: Sul H. Lee) The Haworth Press, Inc., 1993, pp. 19-32. Multiple copies of this article/chapter may be purchased from The Haworth Document Delivery Center [1-800-3-HAWORTH; 9:00 a.m. - 5:00 p.m. (EST)].

© 1993 by The Haworth Press, Inc. All rights reserved.

The forces which can be identified as dominant in the world of academic libraries and publishers in the 1990's, result from global economic trends, from macro-economic conditions in the US, from the massive publishing business restructuring of the 1980's, and from the inherent slowness in responding to change at both the library and publishing communities.

A clear trend of consistent publisher price increases has established itself since the late 1970's. Many explanations and justifications have been offered at times: being a strong US Dollar, a weak US Dollar, high inflation rate at home, high inflation rate abroad, or simply whatever is needed to justify such action. The fact is that for the last fifteen years, prices of books and journals have risen, and always at a rate higher than the overall inflation rate in the world economy. Be it the publishers justifications and explanations, what they may, the impact of these increased trends on libraries, has been an erosion of its purchasing power for both books and journals. Coupled with the consistent pattern of budget and funding cuts over the last seven years, this impact on many libraries has been devastating.

As a result of its very high profitability, the unusually lucrative cash flow, the importance for current research information, and the difficulties associated with subscription cancellations, periodical prices have escalated in an especially rapid manner. The impact of journal subscription price increases has been disproportionate to that of books and other such materials, thus causing significant concern over the growing imbalance in many collections.

In the last three years matters have gotten still worse. While price inflation continued unabated, library operational and acquisitions funds became scarcer, essentially due to state and federal government budget cuts, and reduced support for R & D activities. Forced to cope with such adverse conditions, libraries have begun, though most reluctantly, the process of rationalizing their collections, canceling subscriptions, and reducing their book acquisitions even further.

One would expect, in line with classical marketing and economic theory, that the publishing industry would respond with either substantial price decreases or with a significant downsizing of their publishing programs. In reality, while prices continue to climb, book and journal output not only has not been altered downward to match the decline in the buying power of libraries, it has actually increased in relation to last year and the year before!

This seemingly paradox can be explained in part by the fact that the product development phase in publishing is quite lengthy. The time span from concept to contract may be relatively short, but the period from contract to a published book is inherently long and is not very controllable. The creative processes of writing and editing and the physical one of design, typesetting, printing, and binding, require time and cannot be rushed through without damage. As a result of this product development cycle, publishers are often not synchronized with the economic cycles, over-publishing when the market turns down, and do not respond quickly enough when the demand is high.

Unfortunately this explanation is only partial and is only valid for short term asynchronization with market conditions. To get a better understanding of the more fundamental forces shaping and driving publishing trends and operations we must look at the macro picture.

Most books today are no longer published by relatively small publishers, headed by bibliophiles, driven by the desire to publish worthy works, even when such publishing projects may not always make business sense. Most publishing companies now reflect the results of some fifteen years of consolidations, mergers, and acquisitions. Today, most important publishing companies are either huge publishing concerns who have swallowed and digested numerous small independent publishers, or altogether minor subsidiaries and divisions of major conglomerates, whose interests may cover anything from film and television, to textiles and automotive parts.

The issue here, in the context of publisher-library relationships, is not merely that of ownership, but the business objectives, economic imperatives, and the methods for achieving them, that characterize the "new look" publishing companies.

The process of consolidations, mergers, and acquisitions has brought about several profound changes in the publishing industry, changes which, in turn, affect the library community. Due to the very nature of the "new" publishing company, the key decision making authority is no longer in the hands of the entrepreneurial bibliophile, or in the hands of editorially oriented executives, not even in the hands of marketing oriented managers. Basically, the decision making authority is no longer in the hands of those who have a direct interest and even emotional attachment to the intellectual work itself, people gratified by the creation of a new worthy title. The responsibility for decision making is now in the hands of executives with financial and merchandising background, and a variety of other interests. These decision makers today are likely to view the books and journals of their company as *products*, judging them solely in terms of profitability. In this sense, it matters not to them whether their company produces scholarly books, or shoes, or video games, their interest is rooted in, and their performance is judged by the "bottom line." As such, the publisher is no longer sensitive to and responsive to the needs of the scholarly community, or to the plight of libraries, but to the imperative of "profit and loss" and cash flow considerations.

And these imperatives are powerful indeed. As was the general case with takeovers, mergers, and acquisitions during the "go-go eighties," so it was with this process in the publishing industry. The predatory acquirers did not finance their acquisitions and takeovers from their profits or equity generated funds, but financed it by easily obtained yet most imprudent borrowing on a huge scale. From the stand point of our discussion, the impact of that process today is that most publishing companies are often over-weighted, with a massive burden of debt, and with the all consuming need and stress to generate the income and cash flow required to service this debt. Not much room is left under these circumstances for sympathy to the plight of the library.

Another important point in this context is the issue of orientation and accountability. In the "old style" publishing company the pride of management, its sense of accomplishment, and the measure of its success were a function of achieving its publishing objectives within a reasonably acceptable economic return. Today management is accountable either directly to anonymous stockholders whose interest lies in the return on their investment or the price of their shares, or to corporate financial executives, in their parent conglomerate, who judge performance strictly in terms of financial results, and success in meeting financial objectives.

Another result from the consolidation process of the last fifteen years, quite unfortunate from the standpoint of libraries, or that of adherent classical economic theory, is the creation of publishing monopolies. Almost any area of publishing today, be it scholarly, scientific or technical publications, book and journal publishing, is dominated by a small number of major publishing companies maintaining an overwhelming share of the marketplace. The effect on the library and scholarly communities of this process can be devastating, as publishers, who are also insulated by copyright protection, thus have the added means of controlling the market through restricting competition. This is true not only from their ability to force outrageous pricing practices on libraries, but to control authors and contributors as well, through the limiting of publishing channels available to them.

The transformation of the publishing industry has not been limited to type of ownership and the emergence of virtual publishing monopolies. Publishing has not escaped the fate of so many other American industries and business concerns. It, too, was an important part in the process of the "selling of America." The 1980's, particularly the second half of the decade, were characterized by a weak dollar in relation to most European currencies. To the many European publishing houses, who had been drooling at the prospect of penetrating the lucrative US market, the weak dollar presented a true golden opportunity. To the foreign buyer it was clearly a win-win situation. If the dollar remains weak, they stand to realize handsome return on their cheap investments (in terms of their own currencies). If the dollar gets stronger they stand to realize what will amount to windfall profits, again, in terms of their own currencies. In any event, they have gained, inexpensively, control of major American publishing programs.

The impact of the growth of foreign ownership of American publishing companies may appear, superficially, and to be of little concern. After all, what difference should the ultimate ownership make. But this impact can be most serious because the publisher's decision making process becomes dependent on foreign economies and their needs and conditions, regardless of the library situation and the prevailing economic conditions here in the United States. Unfortunately one does not think much in terms of domestic vs. foreign ownership. Yet, many crucial considerations and decisions have little to do with editorial and production sort of costs, and much to do with the need to generate positive return, in one's own currency and country, on one's investment here in the US.

As has been the case with many other industries that have been victimized by the "selling of America," the process, as it has affected publishing, is not quickly reversible, and certainly not in the near future. Looking further into the future, I see a possible silver lining to this dark cloud. It is conceivable that future changes in relative economic conditions such as significant strengthening of the dollar, may force significant enough distortions of price vs. value, to present attractive opportunities for new entrepreneurial and competitive entries into the publishing field. Scholars are likely to be attracted to these new publishing ventures, because they will present new and innovative approaches to publishing, a welcomed departure from the staid, cumbersome, and expensive practices of "traditional" publishing with their monopolistic controls and unrelenting pressures towards ever higher prices.

Besieged by the dual pressures of relentlessly rising prices of materials on one hand, and the long, multi-year process of budget reduction (a process that, regrettably, does not yet show any sign of abetting), libraries, in search of relief, have been attracted to the one major area of innovation and promise-technology.

Technological progress has been nothing less than spectacular, especially as is evident in the fields of computer technology, including mass storage facilities, and data retrieval capabilities. It is easy, therefore, to understand why the fast pace of continuing technological break-throughs and the sudden availability of capabilities unimagined just a few years ago, have captivated the imagination of many in the library community. Many, in fact, came soon to view technology as a true panacea, the magic potion that will soothe the pains and relieve the struggles.

As is the case with all "panaceas," technology, too, proved not to be a cure-all. It is certainly very important. It has endowed the library with immense new capabilities. It has become an invaluable tool in data management, tracking, and retrieval activities. It has become a crucial tool in the management of the library itself. One thing, however, it has not become—a cure-all!

In its early stages computer technology had a tremendous attraction to business. Being motivated and controlled by the profit motive, businesses viewed computers as a major labor substitute, as a powerful tool in cost reduction, as a source of revenue. It did not take long for the business community to realize that while automation has contributed much in many areas of productivity and to management information and control, it has not reduced the labor force but merely changed it, as it has substituted one category of costs for another.

In the library environment, it was much harder to recognize the shortcomings of technology. It was so because of the enchantment with the promise, with the potential contribution of technology to the library's essential purpose of information management. A critical view of technology and the realization of its shortcomings have only been brought about by the pressure of budget constraints.

There is no question about the fact that computer and peripheral technology allow for storage of monumental volumes of data. More importantly, they provide great capabilities in sifting through this massive store of data and retrieving even the most minute details—a real life analogy for the proverbial search for the needle in the haystack and finding it! Moreover, through telecommunications and networking facilities the library can gain access to a huge and ever expanding array of external databases and information banks.

Why then, with all its capabilities and powerful promise, can we not look forward to technology to provide the solution? Well, in a way it does provide a solution. But, it is a solution to the wrong problem. Technology does provide a most potent tool in matters related to data handling: storage, access, searching, relating, and retrieval. As such, it enhances the library's function as an information center, as a research support resource. It does nothing, however, to solve the key problem currently under discussion, the problem of bridging the gap between the needs of the library and the financial resources available to it. In fact, technology places new demands on the financial resources of the library. Regardless of the accounting and budgetary handling of technology related expenditures, the fact is that technology does cost. To begin with there is the cost of the hardware itself and the inevitable and continuing process of hardware upgrading and expansion. Fortunately hardware costs have been on a long decline enabling the library to achieve more with relatively less. The costs of software, telecommunications, and database connect time are likely, however, to continue their march forward to the point of offsetting and nullifying incurred or anticipated savings.

From the perspective of our discussion, the issue is not whether technology can expand and enhance research and data management capabilities, but, rather, can the library get more for its money through technology. Since any new activity will require new funding, the only possible source of savings from technological applications could come from substituting existing costly activities or acquisitions with much cheaper yet at least as satisfying electronic applications. At present, and in the foreseeable future, the main, if not only, such possibility, is to substitute "paid per use" accessing of electronic data bases for certain journal subscriptions, in the sense of not buying a cow for a glass of milk, but buying the glass of milk itself. Considering the extremely high price of periodical subscriptions to most scientific, technical, and medical journals, this approach appears to be both logical and practical. Alas, it is not. It is not because it is the very same publishers, who control the journals and their subscription prices, including control of the data bases themselves, and of course their accessibility and price. If anything, the amounts spent on information culled from electronic data bases are likely to exceed the savings from the canceled subscriptions themselves. Publishers as would be expected, strive to maintain their overall revenue levels, and to enhance it by exploiting the growing need and desire for electronic data accessing and retrieval.

It is practically an axiom that human endeavor is driven by scarcity: Scarcity of economic resources, scarcity of time, of space, of focus and finally we move to scarcity of patience. In a world sometimes of plenty, there is hardly a need to agonize through planning, to suffer through execution, and to worry about things to come. If not for scarcity of resources we surely would not be here today discussing the issue of declining acquisitions budgets.

I tend to view the 1970's, especially the early part of the decade, as the period in which the situation of the academic library was as close to ideal as it could get, particularly from the perspective of collection diversity, development, and balance. This was a period in which the resources available to libraries were adequate for pursuing collection objectives without compromise. It was generally a period in which supply, in terms of what publishers made available, was in balance with the demand generated by library collection policies. It was the period before a steep linear growth in the numbers and an exponential jump in the cost of publishing products distorted the desired balance in the collections of libraries. A distortion made worse by a continuing, often accelerating process of funding cuts and budgetary constraints.

As stated earlier, the one development that impacted library acquisitions practices most brutally, was the dramatic rise in the cost of periodical subscriptions. Caught short by both suddenness and scale of the increases, libraries did not have enough time to respond to the swift changes by considering the effects on their collections, or reconsidering their buying policies and adjusting them to the new reality. Unprepared, the libraries succumbed to the new conditions by allocating a greater portion of their acquisitions funds to journal subscriptions in order to maintain the continuity and completeness of their periodicals collection.

To the publishing industry, the library's response, or rather lack of a more assertive response, was an eye opener. The industry discovered that their most profitable product line by far, is also the one that the library must maintain virtually with no regard to costs. The natural result was a quantitative explosion in journal publishing, fed on one hand by publisher's appetite, and on the other by academic communities desperate urge to "publish or perish."

The effect on the library's collection planning was devastating. Not given time to gather its wits, the library was pummeled by the triple punch of steeply rising prices, the ever continuing rise in the volume of material, and steeply declining funds. Thus denied the opportunity to influence events and coerced into assuming a weak reactive stance, there was little the library could do more than bemoan its travails and shift an ever growing share of its purchasing funds to the very temporary satisfaction of what was swiftly becoming a ravenous periodicals "monster."

The ineffective response of the library to the triple edged assault upon it has resulted from a true weakness and not because it has failed to appreciate and focus on the real issues and the real dangers.

Moreover, the changes that have been forced on the library for more than a decade now have heightened the sense in the library that it has to regain control over its course, that it has to redefine its priorities, and that it has to find an appropriate way to reassert itself.

The key professional issue facing the library is determining the desired nature of its collection, and the definition of its collection development objectives. And, the reassessment of the relative value of the various components of its collection, particularly that of books vs. journals, while developing the tools and means to achieve them. The distortion brought about by the ascendancy of journals in the last fifteen years or so, has brought into sharper focus the fact that books are the essence of a library collection, that books are characterized by their lasting quality while journals are ephemeral by their very nature, and their value is determined by the current demand, generated by the currency of the data they contain, while their archival value is low, even when they are new and is almost non-existent within a short period of time.

Books, on the other hand, do not deal much with data but with organized information. They are oriented towards understanding rather than description, towards intellectual speculation rather than empirical findings, towards the whole rather than the parts. Therefore, the most sensible approach is to determine the desirable balance in a collection by discipline. Certain disciplines, such as: business, fine Arts, literature, history, and philosophy are clearly book oriented, while the many technological and scientific areas rely much more heavily on the kind of information and research data contained in current periodicals.

It is my opinion, that the potential for savings from substituting electronic data access for journal subscriptions is quite limited, certainly much more limited than what may seem apparent at first. The reason is rooted in the very process of intellectual inquiry that depends on the casual perusal of information, on the "aimless" leafing through the pages for the sudden insight, for the crystallization of a problem, for seeing the "macro." Even the most extensive data base and the most refined method of searching and retrieval cannot substitute for this casual perusal of information, not data. I, therefore, expect that only a limited number of journals, mostly scientific in nature, can be replaced satisfactorily by electronic access methods.

I hope that in this presentation I was able to touch upon some of the key issues from their long-term perspectives. The essence is that the situation of the library, in terms of its control over its collection, has worsened progressively for many years and is not going to improve dramatically. The traditional remedies of lobbying for funds and/or cutting expenditures on important aspects of the collection, have lost any effectiveness. Even though relief budget injections are possible from time to time, they are not going to do anything more than bring occasional, temporary, symptomatic relief.

What can be done then? How can the library address this problem?

The answer, in my opinion is to change its view of itself internally and change its posture externally.

The library is the largest single budget center in any academic organization, and nowhere else in it, is anyone given the authority and responsibility to control vast amounts of funds, coupled with the charter and freedom to expand such sums in collecting and compiling a body of knowledge that is at the very core of the institution. In the true fulfillment of its function, the library faces the very same kinds of pressure, problems, and imperatives that are faced by any business entity. True, the library's primary purpose is not to generate profit, but its way of achieving its own purpose is subjected to the application of the same principles and the same elements of management theory. The library cannot view itself as a passive and reactive "non-profit" organization, but as an active, dynamic, and assertive organization whose aim is to seize the initiative in the pursuit of its objectives.

Unfortunately not very many libraries are in a position to generate their own revenue. Much can be done, however, to control expenses while pursuing their collection development goals. To succeed in its quest, the library must first define the purpose and the objectives of its collection. This accomplished, each library, or group of libraries, should give much thought and consideration to the optimal balance in their collection by kind of material, by type and format of publications, and by allowing for anticipated future developments. Obviously, the "ideal" balance variations can be extreme from subject to subject and from library to library—as would be the case, for example, in comparing fine arts or philosophy collections with those of, say, mathematics or engineering—the process of establishing the desirable balance must cover discipline by discipline, be done very carefully and comprehensively, and give full weight to the wishes of the users.

Once established, the library's formalized "Statement of Optimized Collection," must be "formulized" and/or codified into a clear rigid formula embodying the library's collection objectives.

This formula will become the library's most potent weapon in its struggle to control prices and keep them within reasonable range. The library community as a whole, and, of course, each individual library, must commit themselves to strict adherence to their formula, thus issuing a simple yet firm and powerful statement and message to the publishing industry. This formula represents the library's policy on the future development of the collection. Funds are limited so we must spend them in strict accordance with the balance formula. If the price of any component rises disproportionately to others it will result in an automatic cancellation so that other collection areas do not suffer. In essence, now is the time for action and the movement away from reacting.

There is a very comforting element in concentrating on the *micro*. We deal with a set of problems with which we are very familiar. We have in our arsenal an array of tried and tested weapons which we can wield with confidence. We know the players involved, we master the techniques, we can anticipate the consequences of our moves and decisions. Unfortunately, those events and the processes that truly affect our overall condition and situation, occur at the *macro* level subject to the *law of unintended consequences*. Viewing matters from the macro point of view is, of course, very complex and quite uncertain, yet important conclusions can be drawn and useful guidelines for positive action charted.

Regretably, the only dubious comfort that can be gleaned from the macro picture, is that, the kind of problems faced by us are shared by all, in the sense of "misery likes company." The entire world is in the grip of economic recession, where weak economies are devastated and stronger economies reflect little or no growth, or even suffer major reversals. The short term prospects for significant improvement are not very good to begin with, when considered in the context of the global political situation. While the end of the Cold War created high expectations of a relaxed political atmosphere which would encourage peace, prosperity, and cooperation, in reality no appreciable change has occurred. In fact, it is quite possible that if there was some "world misery index" such index would indicate worsening political conditions, spreading hunger, expanding poverty, and ever dwindling natural resources. Using the same basic analytical approach, we can easily deduce that the global political arena is as dangerous and worrisome as ever before. In actuality, the major, yet well defined and usually containable threat from the former Soviet Union, has been replaced by a plethora of "mini" threats from a dizzying variety of sources and geographical quarters. The new Director of the CIA, during his recent confirmation hearings described the situation quite succinctly by saying: "The dragon has been slain, but now the jungle is teeming with a huge number of poisonous snakes." Indeed from Somalia to Cambodia, from Bosnia to Armenia, from Angola to Iraq, there is nothing but warfare, insecurity, suffering, fear, hunger, and death.

Not only is the global picture rather dark and dismaying, but the domestic picture too, although inherently so different, does not indicate major and significant improvements in the short term. An important aspect of the domestic perspective is that, in general, we elect to political offices, at all levels of government, from the federal down to the municipal level, people who are essentially inept. This assertion, is not meant to be of the all-encompassing type, and there are, of course, in government, many people outstanding in vision, ability, and performance, but all too often the better qualified and the more capable people choose not to join the political process, and as a result we are left with mediocrity among the ranks of what should constitute our leadership.

The issues of our enormous cumulative national debt and our mind-boggling annual budget deficits are much more profound than the merely direct economic effect. They do, in fact, reflect the deep changes in the kind of a country we are, the type of society we live in, and in our expectations for the future. Further, when our budget deficits are viewed together with our trade deficits, they demonstrate quite clearly that the foundations of our economic structure have changed profoundly, and probably irreversibly, by the erosion of our competitive manufacturing advantage and by our growing reliance on imported energy.

Dealing with these issues and problems demand bold and courageous steps that are a blend of the visionary and the prudent, the revolutionary and the conservative simultaneously. In other words, it requires truly exceptional and outstanding leadership. Unfortunately the mediocrity in leadership ranks that the world political process has produced, does not allow me to be overly optimistic and entertain expectations of dramatic, speedy, and profound improvements in our economic state. On the contrary, I expect that working our way out of the current recession will be the easy part. Only then will we be in a position to start tackling our real problems.

As we return to the *micro* perspective, we find that, inescapably, the economic situation of the library (and the library's various suppliers) is an integral part of the *Macro*. It is a part not only of the regional or national picture but a reflection of the global situation as well.

I believe that in the last 15-20 years, perhaps in conjunction with economic reality, education as a whole has declined from its high position on our scale of social priorities. The library, being an integral part of the educational institution, has suffered from the same fate. Unfortunately, because such a decline is a subtle and very gradual process, it was impossible to focus on it and respond accordingly. Instead, the educational system as a whole, and the library as one of its important parts, have hurt a generation by trying to deal with profound, long-term developments as if they were problems that may respond to short-term solutions.

In conclusion, I must state that I am a person who always maintains an optimum viewpoint. Although my paper delivered here today appears to paint a rather bleak picture of the world economy, I really do not see it that way. However, what I do see and believe is that we must take a hard realistic look at all of the issues and problems, accept them, analyze them, and come up with an achievable plan, and finally put that plan into action and grow.

# Crisis and Opportunity: Reevaluating Acquisitions Budgeting in an Age of Transition

Ross Atkinson

The academic library has but one purpose, and that is to support the educational and scholarly objectives of the institution it serves. The new information era we are now gradually entering, however, calls into question the ability of the library's traditional operations to support those institutional objectives. The continued participation of the library in the academic enterprise will therefore depend increasingly on the facility with which the library is able systematically to replace those current operations—on the basis of which it has defined its existence for so many decades—with new ones that will be able to respond more effectively to the new information needs and expectations of higher education. The many challenges the academic library presently faces in the current environment, including especially the endemic erosion of library resources, must be confronted and can be overcome, therefore, only within this context of transition.

Certainly one of the most visible and highly publicized economic challenges facing the academic library at this time is the decline in the purchasing power of the acquisitions budget. Large-scale serial

---

Ross Atkinson is Assistant University Librarian, Collection Development and Preservation, Cornell University, Ithaca, NY.

[Haworth co-indexing entry note]: "Crisis and Opportunity: Reevaluating Acquisitions Budgeting in an Age of Transition." Atkinson, Ross. Co-published simultaneously in *Journal of Library Administration* (The Haworth Press, Inc.) Vol. 19, No. 2, 1993, pp. 33-55; and: *Declining Acquisitions Budgets: Allocation, Collection Development and Impact Communication* (ed: Sul H. Lee) The Haworth Press, Inc., 1993, pp. 33-55. Multiple copies of this article/chapter may be purchased from The Haworth Document Delivery Center [1-800-3-HAWORTH; 9:00 a.m. - 5:00 p.m. (EST)].

© 1993 by The Haworth Press, Inc. All rights reserved.

cancellation projects have become a way of life for all academic libraries. The prices of many library materials are growing much more rapidly than library acquisition budgets, which has led to an increasingly evident degradation in the quality and depth of library collections in all types and sizes of academic institutions.[1]

Major efforts by libraries to combat this decline have been directed primarily outward in the form of public denunciations of publisher prices and of overtures to other libraries to establish cooperative or coordinated acquisition agreements. Neither of these tactics has proven very successful–partially, in my opinion, because of the competitiveness and internal fragmentation of the academic community and the academic library. This is not to claim, of course, that adjustments to relationships within and among academic institutions and their libraries will lead miraculously to a decline in externally imposed costs of library materials, but rather only that such adjustments must form an essential first step toward the creation of a practicable strategy to manage the costs of scholarly communication during this period of transition. The purpose of this paper, therefore, will be to consider why and how the acquisitions budget should for that purpose be integrated into the broader library and institutional budgetary and planning process.

## THE COLLECTION DEVELOPMENT ETHOS

Research library collection development in its modern form evolved in the 1960s as a kind of organizational and political mitosis. Inside the library, collection development disengaged itself from the processing side of library operations–principally the acquisitions function–basing this separation on the distinction between selection and acquisition. This led to the division of the academic library into its current tripartite structure of public services, technical services, and collection development. At the same time, academic library collection development defined itself outside of the library by assuming responsibilities previously in the hands of some faculty users.[2] This process was undertaken deliberately but gradually–aided by such innovations as the modern collection policy, which in its early form doubtless functioned as a kind of guarantee or assurance to faculty that their bibliographic needs would be effectively met even after they themselves were no longer initiating selection decisions. This assumption of responsibility was possible and necessary at least partially because of the fundamental fragmentation of the faculty. One purpose of collection development, therefore, has always been in effect to provide a form of adjudication in order to ensure that the bibliographic resources needed by different faculty users and programs would be equitably distributed. Fulfilling this responsibility—and indeed retaining the authority for fulfilling it—will admittedly become increasingly difficult in an age in which users interact directly with information online.

The essential instrument that drives and sustains collection development has always been the acquisitions budget. Outside the library, the budget permits collection development to respond to faculty needs and to function as an equitable distributor of bibliographic resources. Inside the library, it is at least partially by means of the acquisitions budget that collection development is able to guide and influence library policy. "The form the budget takes, and the process used to achieve it, . . . reflect the decision-making authority within the library."[3] In the same way that different faculty groups or members are in frequent competition for institutional resources, different segments of the library are also often unavoidably in some form of competition with each other. The budgetary authority of collection development, combined with its close linkage to faculty, has empowered it to play a role equal and complementary to the more established functions of public services and technical services.[4]

Competition among different library operations is understandably exacerbated by austerity. "What heightens competition most of all is the perception of a finite sum of money to allocate."[5] Because library resources are so clearly in a state of decline, they are as such inadequate to support properly all library operations. Each operation naturally assumes its contribution to information services is among the most critical and therefore deserves preferential treatment. What is different about collection development is that in its case this preferential treatment has often been forthcoming. In many institutions, the acquisitions budget is maintained separately from the rest of the library's budget, because of its perceived significance, and in order to counteract the traditionally higher level of inflation for library materials. This convention of a separate acquisitions budget has also contributed to collection development's autonomy. The university administration further strengthens this autonomy by stipulating often that funding allocated for materials is to be spent for no other purpose. The administration recognizes, moreover, that the acquisitions budget is–theoretically–a source of value to the entire institution, and therefore represents a safe and nonpartisan budget increase even (or especially) in times of austerity. Such preferential treatment of the acquisitions budget, it must be admitted, may result in part from a misunderstanding of the information services process by the institutional administration: the implication seems to be that the acquisitions budget must be protected–even, if necessary, at the expense of staff and library infrastructure, as if information sources could be made accessible merely by purchasing them. This is obviously absurd, yet to deny this assumption too vigorously might well result in the library receiving no preferential treatment from the institution at all. The end result has been in any event that collection development budgetary resources have increased much more rapidly than those of other library operations–possibly to the detriment of information services as a whole.

*The Library as Agency.* All well functioning service organizations, including especially information services, understand themselves to be representatives of their clientele. All academic librarians see themselves more or less as agents of their users. The library is therefore in many respects an agency, in the narrow sense of an organization created and sustained for the sole purpose of acting in the interest of some group other than itself. We do well to bear in mind, therefore, as G. Stevenson Smith points out, the existence of a substantial literature on agency theory, a basic premise of which is that agencies sometimes unwittingly or even perhaps intentionally tend to act in their own self-interest, rather than in the interests of their principals or clients.[6] In order to avoid such situations, contracts are agreed upon between agents and their principals. In academic libraries, budgets and collection policies presumably serve those same contractual purposes.

Let me stress at once that I do not mean to imply that collection development has ever intentionally acted in its own self-interest or has ever intended to misrepresent anyone, including especially the institution or faculty it serves. We must admit at the same time, however, that the function of research library collection development has gained somewhat in significance as a direct result of the so-called serials crisis. Demonstrable scarcity increases budgets, and it increases the authority of budget managers. Nowhere in the library is scarcity as visible or as easily demonstrated as in collection building. Indeed, the costs of library materials (due in part to the price increases of European science publishers) are increasing so rapidly that no university could ever expand the library's acquisitions budget year after year at a rate which could even begin to keep pace with such price increases.

This condition of demonstrably declining purchasing power has been evident now in the acquisitions budget for the better part of two decades—in other words, for practically as long as collection development has been in existence. It is especially important therefore that we begin to recognize that collection development, both as a library function and as a political entity, is at least in part a product of this seemingly inexorable budgetary decline. Collection development is in its modern form inseparable from, and perhaps now even inconceivable without, the decline in library resources in general and the serials crisis in particular. Collection development has defined itself, established its goals, and measured its successes mainly in terms of that decline. Collection development has in fact become that library (or information service) function which seeks to build collections and to provide access to information in an environment of inadequate resources and negligible control over the means of publication production. Again, I certainly do not mean to imply that collection development either desired or conspired to create this condition. I am saying, however, that collection development would be a very different function in the absence of those extreme budgetary pressures typified by the serials crisis. It is important to understand therefore that the successful eradication of those factors that have created such budgetary pressures will fundamentally alter the profession of collection development administration.

*The Pursuit of Cooperation.* Of the several courses of action which collection development has considered to alleviate this condition, certainly the most visible and perhaps most innately logical has been cooperative collection development. Several versions and theories of cooperative collection development have evolved, but certainly the best known and most discussed has been the synergistic version, in which different libraries take responsibility for collecting different publications, according to some coordinated plan. The most successful instance of such synergism was surely the Farmington Plan, which was intended to divide responsibilities for the selection and acquisition of foreign publications.[7] The effort to apply that same process to the acquisition of higher use materials, such as science journals, was, as Richard Dougherty and others have since pointed out, somewhat flawed from the beginning–if for no other reason than that, if we succeeded in dividing such responsibility for expensive serials among institutions, this would reduce the total number of subscriptions, which would in turn almost certainly encourage the publishers of those serials to increase subscription rates, thus eliminating any savings for the libraries participating in such a strategy.[8] The cancellation of expensive, commercially produced serials, in other words, will not reduce costs, because it will generally result in the increase in the prices of those remaining commercially produced serials to which the library continues to subscribe. As long as the library does not control publication production, it will not control costs. The large science publishers, who account for an increasing proportion of that production, will demand increasing revenues, regardless of how academic libraries divide selection responsibilities among themselves. The copyright laws also conspire against cooperative collection development, because the publishers are of course intelligent enough to charge higher prices for their higher use materials–and if we were to cancel such high use items, we would doubtless end up borrowing them so frequently through interlibrary loan that we would be legally compelled to resubscribe.

But these are not the only reasons we have failed to put broad cooperative collection development programs into effect. Indeed, we have seldom brought our cooperative planning far enough even to test these assumptions, although we have discussed and analyzed cooperative collection development from every conceivable angle. Perhaps the most extended and certainly one of the most energetic and altruistic efforts to create a national cooperative collection development program was the Research Libraries Group Collection Management and Development Committee. This group, which included during its existence many of the best minds in research library collection development, met at first quarterly, and then biannually for over a decade. It was supported and encouraged financially and morally by many of the largest research institutions in the nation, and it examined cooperative collection development from many perspectives. It devised detailed plans, and it worked industriously to put those plans into effect. Some of those efforts–notably the group's greatest monument, the Conspectus–but also some other programs, such as the Long Term Serials Project–are still in operation and still have some influence. But it must be admitted that the calculable effect of this decade of effort on the acquisitions budgets of the participating institutions, when compared especially with the cost of the Committee's operation, were probably negligible. There are many reasons for this, including most notably the inability of any institution to participate successfully in any program that entails the purchase of materials needed by scholars at another institution at the expense of materials needed by its own users. One further reason for the inability of CMDC to develop more effective cooperative programs may have been that the RLG program committees were designed to mirror the academic libraries they were intended to support. Separate committees were formed, therefore, for collection development, technical services, public services, and preservation, thus perpetuating the divisions among those primary library functions and impairing further their coordination. While the CMDC, moreover, worked hard and long on a unified collection policy, the Conspectus, a unified budgeting process was seldom if ever considered. This inability or unwillingness to reconsider or revise local budgeting methods, which do indeed reflect "the values and priorities of the library, and of the broader institution itself,"[9] bears witness both to the inability of libraries to transcend their internal divisions and to their reluctance to look beyond their own walls for the potential provision of traditional library services to their local clientele.

*Using What We Have.* In the absence of control over key sources of library expenses, including especially publication production, the library must at the very least ensure that it is making optimum use of what resources it does have at its disposal. This will require, first, some mechanism that allows, or indeed forces, the library routinely to consider cooperative programs of all types with other institutions. Some process for quantifying and assessing the cost benefits of cooperation, and of regularly comparing the benefits of cooperation with those of independence must be put in place. Second, the optimum use of library resources will require greater participation of clientele in decisions as to how resources are to be used. We must expect this expanded participation to develop in any event as users become increasingly able to obtain access to information electronically without using the library directly. If the library is to continue to fulfill its function as both intermediary and adjudicator, if it is to move successfully at all through the age of transition it is now entering, better opportunity for faculty participation in–or at least observation of–the resource allocation process must be provided. Third, and equally important, the optimum use of library resources requires within the library the creation of library-wide priorities, and the application of those priorities across library functions–or more exactly: it will require the ability (a) to determine which aspects of which library functions will contribute most effectively to the fulfillment of those priorities, and then (b) to support those functions accordingly. Such an expansion of the resource allocation process inside and outside the library threatens the autonomy and authority of collection development more than any other library function–and it is precisely for this reason that collection development must initiate this process.

## *REMODELING THE LIBRARY BUDGET*

The primary instrument for this transformation must be the budget. We must adopt budgeting methods that will permit us to use the budget as a planning tool and as a communications device. Several methods have been devised to respond to such needs, but few have proven satisfactory.[10] Program Planning and Budgeting, while an arguably effective budgeting method for the Department of Defence thirty years ago, has been very difficult to apply in many other organizations, including libraries. Zero-base budgeting has been somewhat more effective, and remains potentially applicable to some library budgeting needs.[11] Whatever method is selected, however, it is essential that the budget project the true costs of academic information services, and that it clarify the priorities the library intends to adopt in order to meet those costs. In collection development, we have in the past relied primarily on written collection development policies to achieve some of these purposes. Collection policies are, however, often difficult for faculty (or indeed for anyone outside of collection development) to understand easily, and they remain in any event meaningless abstractions for staff and faculty alike when not directly connected to the budget. The other major drawback of collection policies is that they can also serve to isolate (or insulate) collection development from other equally essential library services which directly affect access. While a collection policy may therefore guide or reflect the library's selection of materials, it only partially regulates their accessibility to users, because the policy does not necessarily stipulate the priorities of other library functions.[12]

Both the collection policy and the materials budget in their current forms, therefore, can lead to a fragmentation of library operations: the policy and the budget give the impression—propound the illusion—that different library operations are undertaken for different purposes—rather than that all library operations are merely different methods, or links in a chain, to achieve the single purpose of local access. If the fragmentation of the academic research library into separate and competing jurisdictions is to be even somewhat alleviated, therefore, fundamental redistributions and redefinitions of operational authority and responsibility throughout the library system may need to be effected. Care must be taken in any event to avoid a condition in which different traditional library operations are perceived and run as relatively separate enterprises, each with its own self-defined objectives. We must consequently redesign and learn to use the library budget to serve not only as a communications vehicle with the institution but also as a process to bring about a more effective coordination and coalescence of traditional library operations.

Our immediate goals should be therefore (a) to foster a reintegration of the acquisitions budget with the full library budget, so that the true costs and cost benefits of library services and information access will be apparent, (b) to extend the collection policy into a full library operational policy, defining priorities in unified terms for all library "selection" activities, including especially cataloging, ILL, location (off-site storage), and preservation as well as collection building, and (c) finally to amalgamate this expanded budget and this expanded policy into a single document that will engage the library, the user community, and the institutional administration in the planning and budgeting process, that will promote the assessment of potential cooperative programs with other institutions and that will support the gradual transformation of academic information services. This is admittedly a tall order—but one upon which the future effectiveness of academic information services directly depends. I will spend the remainder of this paper making a few suggestions as to how the first step in this process—budget integration—might be achieved.

*Multidimensional Budgeting.* Academic libraries need to look more to the commercial sector for organizational and budgetary models. In our exasperation over what we view as our exploitation by commercial publishers, we have failed to appreciate their success. Their purpose is to make money, and we must admit they have achieved that purpose spectacularly. We must not be repelled by the commercial sector, therefore, but should rather study and learn from it, even though the objectives of academic libraries often diverge significantly from those of commerce. One innovation recently proposed for larger businesses is what Jeffrey A. Schmidt calls multidimensional budgeting, the purpose of which is to convert "conventional budgets into formats that are more relevant to management."[13] Schmidt suggests four separate budgets, or budget dimensions: an activity budget, a product budget, a customer budget, and a strategy budget, each of which is connected or mapped onto the previous one.

> ... management can assess resource allocations by working down from the strategic budget to the base conventional budget. At each level, management can test the correct alignment of resources against its priorities, and the budget can be adjusted, as necessary, until an optimal statement is achieved.[14]

Certainly multidimensional budgeting is intended to achieve some of the main goals as the planning-programming-budget system and zero-base budgeting, especially in its aim to use budgeting as a means to establish priorities—but multidimensional budgeting is not nearly as complex and exacting a process as PPBS or ZBB. It is rather, in my opinion, simply a call to look at the same funding from a variety of successive perspectives, in order to learn more about the rationale for past expenditures and to understand more clearly the implications of potential allocation decisions. Viewed from another perspective, multidimensional budgeting, which some companies, or even some libraries, may well be practicing in one form or another already, is merely a method to move systematically from an incremental budget to one which better reflects programs and policy.

How might multidimensional budgeting be applied in academic libraries? To be sure, with some difficulty. Not only is the redefinition of budget categories a problematic and potentially controversial undertaking, but such categories must also permit accounting procedures to be devised that will permit the capture of appropriate expenditure data. Such challenges must nevertheless be confronted, if the budget is to serve as a mechanism for communication and functional integration.

In designing a multidimensional budgetary model for libraries, we could try to adopt Schmidt's four budget dimensions to library purposes; it is probably preferable, however, to define our own dimensions. Most academic libraries will presumably want be to shown how library services support academic programs, and they will want the budget to provide insights and facilitate decisions on how the costs of those services should be distributed. We need therefore to move through a minimum of three dimensions: from (a) the traditional operating budget through (b) a service budget to (c) some kind of program or policy budget. The process of mapping one budget on to the next will necessarily strain some budget categories, and will require that some of these categories be modified. This categorical review and redefinition should be accepted, however, as an inevitable and ultimately beneficial consequence of any planning effort. We will therefore develop a budget with three budget dimensions, each of which should be used in order to allocate *the same* available funding. (The grand total of each budget dimension, in other words, should be the same.) The same categories should be used to record expenses, of course, both to track spending and to produce historical information that can be applied to future allocation decisions.

*First Dimension: The Operational Budget.* We will list the budget categories on the vertical axis, and the cost (or "responsibility") centers on the horizontal axis (see Figure 1). Most academic libraries will use some version of this traditional line-item budget. Funding is allocated by category to the cost centers, each of which has a budget manager responsible for suballocation and expenditures. The cost centers in the standard library budget are often library units–individual libraries in the system or central departments. Each cost center then has its own subbudget within which it will define its own budget categories. When there is a separate collection development operation, of course, the materials budget is suballocated, usually by subject.[15] We will use the standard budget categories of personnel, materials and "other," in which the latter often refers increasingly to online services. As Werking has shown, the "other" category has been growing more rapidly in academic libraries than the categories of materials and personnel.[16]

This standard form of budgeting provides considerable flexibility–with the notable exception that many libraries are prohibited by their central administrations from shifting funds between materials and personnel. The independent authority given to individual fund managers, moreover, shields much of the use of the operational budget from external scrutiny, protecting it from many outside pressures, and ensuring that the administrative integrity of the library budget remains intact.[17] For these same reasons, however, the standard operational budget is not very helpful for purposes of planning or communication. The real application of the budget takes place

|  | Main Library | Branch 1 | Branch 2 | Central Processing | TOTAL |
|---|---|---|---|---|---|
| Personnel |  |  |  |  |  |
| Materials |  |  |  |  |  |
| Other |  |  |  |  |  |
| TOTAL |  |  |  |  |  |

Figure 1. Operations Budget.

relatively out of sight, so that the transformation of fiscal resources into information services is obscured. While this can be seen to safeguard the library's autonomy, it also makes it difficult to argue for increased funding—or even to explain how changes in allocation affect the availability and utility of information to meet the scholarly and instructional needs of the institution. While the standard operations budget remains essential as a first budgeting step and should be retained, the budgeting process should not be concluded with such a budget. A more effective budgeting mechanism is also required, therefore, by means of which the uses of the budget can be displayed more visibly. This should be the purpose of the service budget.

*Second Dimension: The Service Budget.* I would suggest that the service budget be mapped onto the operational budget by retaining the same budget categories, replacing the units with services as the cost centers, and then rebudgeting the amounts in the final column of the operational budget across the new service budget.[18] The process of designating services as cost centers is of critical importance, because these will be viewed by the institutional community as the primary justifications for the library's maintenance and support. The library will in effect define itself through these categories. Whatever services the library decides to select, they should be understandable or easily explainable to users, and they should be adaptable to transition, i.e., simultaneously applicable to both traditional and online services.

I am convinced that the major service division in the library must be between mediation (which encompasses the traditional functions of reference, collection development, and cataloging) and delivery (e.g., acquisitions, circulation, ILL, preservation, library systems).[19] I would therefore aim to divide all services into these general categories as soon as possible, although certainly more traditional categories may be initially preferable for most libraries.[20] Since we must account for the entire budget in each dimension, we are compelled to add a third cost center, which is not a service, but which nevertheless must be supported: administration. The administrative budget should be kept on principle to a minimum in order to ensure that most budgetary decisions and uses are effected at the service level, and to avoid using the administrative category as a catch-all to evade the chore of distinguishing between the operational service categories.

An important part of any budget as a planning or management tool must be the consideration of alternatives or options. These might be added to the service budget as subcategories. Such options should be included, it seems to me, in any planning budget, even if some of them are not used. In such cases, the amount allocated for unaccepted options is simply zero, but the option should remain in the budget as a record of the decision, and so that the possible use of that option in future can be revisited. Many different kinds of alternative options might be included. The development of alternatives should promote discussions not only of adjusted or improved services, but also of so-called "opportunity costs," i.e., those activities or opportunities that will be forfeited by selecting one option over another.[21] For the purposes of our example, let us consider the fundamental alternative between funding something internally and contracting it out to an external agency. We will therefore include the simple (and oversimplified) options of "internal" and "external" as subcategories in our services budget example (see Figure 2).

Care must obviously be taken in defining "external services"—specifically, whether this refers to operations external to the library or external to the institution. In my opinion, which is admittedly based on experience in larger academic institutions, it is preferable to define "external services" as external to the library, thus encour-

|  | Mediation | Delivery | Administration | TOTAL |
|---|---|---|---|---|
| Personnel Internal |  |  |  |  |
| External |  |  |  |  |
| Materials Internal |  |  |  |  |
| External |  |  |  |  |
| Other Internal |  |  |  |  |
| External |  |  |  |  |
| TOTAL Internal |  |  |  |  |
| External |  |  |  |  |

Figure 2. Service Budget.

aging comparisons between the costs of institutional services and those of agencies outside the institution. So long as the library's budget is separate from that of the rest of the institution, whether one transfers funds to another campus operation or to a distant commercial enterprise makes no difference to the budget (although it may to the institution).

We now begin to perceive the first strains on our standard budget categories. Using external personnel for administrators, for example, while certainly a tantalizing idea, is probably not very practicable. On the other hand, such a budget format would encourage some estimation of the cost benefits of using external staff for some mediation services: cataloging or selection or even reference. The more we advance into the online era, the more feasible will become the use of external staff for such purposes. The same is true, of course, for the various services that come under the heading of delivery: while today most delivery staff will no doubt be in the library, the storage and delivery of online information will be increasingly contracted out or shared among institutions. This should be reflected and anticipated in the budget.

The most problematic category is no doubt materials, by which we mean publications regardless of format that are read or accessed primarily by library users–but arguably also by library staff. Materials that fall within the mediation category include those that identify or describe or refer to other materials, i.e., reference sources. These sources–e.g., bibliographies, indexes–should be understood as falling primarily in the external option category. This is important: we must recognize that we are in effect contracting out to publishers for the production of such sources. There is, on the other hand, one large and expensive reference publication that is now produced internally, which is the library catalog. We notice at once, however, that the cost of the catalog as a publication manifests itself primarily in the cost of the staff producing it. In other words, most internal costs for the production of materials would normally appear in the budget as personnel costs. Materials costs are therefore probably by definition external, and I would recommend that we include all non-reference library materials in the category of external delivery, because all publications are fundamentally delivery mechanisms that have been in a sense contracted out to external agencies (for the most part, to publishers).

It is in this category of external delivery, then, that the enormous costs of materials–the origin of the serials crisis, and of much of the decline in the fiscal resources of the library generally–are located in the budget. The structure of the budget should force the institution therefore to recognize publication–especially commercial publication–as essentially an external, contracted service; the budget should further require us to consider, as we did in the case of personnel, the potential cost implications of shifting those costs or allocations from, in this case, external to internal. By generating an initially somewhat contradictory category of "internal materials" (which would admittedly ultimately manifest itself as an internal personnel cost), the service budget compels us to consider this as an alternative delivery mechanism–not on the airy theoretical level, but on the highly practical level of budget allocation. Each time the budget process is enacted, therefore, the prospects of a shift from external to internal–from commercial to local, institutional publication–will or should be weighed. The further we move into the online age, the more opportunities to transfer delivery responsibilities from external publishers to the institution (or preferably the library) will become apparent.[22] And the more open the budgeting process, the more users who need publications to be delivered to them (and who want their own publications delivered to others) will be made aware of these opportunities.

Administrative materials, to complete our review of the service budget categories, might consist mainly of management information, some of it produced externally, and some internally.[23] Access to this information is increasingly important for research library management, but its costs are rarely articulated, and the resources needed to create it are seldom clearly allocated. Finally, the "other" category will consist of the same kinds of items as those in the operational budget–mainly supplies and equipment–except that one might prefer to budget bibliographic utility fees–e.g., for OCLC and RLIN–not in the "other" category in the services budget, but rather as an external mediation cost for materials.

*Third Dimension: The Program Budget.* In order to map the service budget to the program budget, I would suggest using the previously identified services as the new budget categories, then defining the programs as the new cost centers. This will involve taking the final row of costs (total) in the service budget and rebudgeting those costs across the new budget, so that the final column in the program budget will be identical to the final row in the service budget. The purpose of the program budget is to shift the perspective from the information service programs, as conveyed in the service budget, to the client or institutional programs.[24] How such programs are designated in the budget depends upon the values and priorities of the individual institution, and upon the message the library wants to convey to its clientele community. Obviously the users themselves need to identify with the programs listed–to understand the needs and capacities with which they are affiliated–so probably the most effective approach might be simply to use the administrative divisions within the institution, such as colleges or departments.[25]

For purposes of our example, let us simply use as our programmatic cost centers the standard subject categories of humanities, social sciences, sciences, and interdisciplinary (see Figure 3). Ideally we might prefer in many instances to budget information service costs across other cost centers, for example: instruction, current research, long-term/potential research. Instruction and research are certainly the two most frequently cited divisions of institutional programmatic responsibilities, and if we could divide research into

| | Humanities | Social Science | Sciences | Interdiciplinary | TOTAL |
|---|---|---|---|---|---|
| Mediation Internal | | | | | |
| External | | | | | |
| Delivery Internal | | | | | |
| External | | | | | |
| Administration Internal | | | | | |
| External | | | | | |
| TOTAL Internal | | | | | |
| External | | | | | |

Figure 3. Program Budget.

current (needed now for ongoing research) and long-term (needed potentially in future to maintain quality collections), this would provide a fine opportunity to establish funding priorities: we could demonstrate that, as purchasing power erodes, we must shift costs increasingly from long-term to current research, and then from current research to instructional support. We could use what we budget for long-term research as a basis for cooperative collection development programs. Such categories might also be useful for calculating indirect costs for federal grants, which often support materials acquired for research, but not for instruction. While this may appear to be a reasonable budgetary structure in theory, however, anyone who has tried it must readily admit that it is highly problematic in reality, because we cannot in most cases determine whether materials acquired and cataloged will be used for instruction or research. Materials acquired for graduate instruction, for example, are often the same as those used for faculty research–and whether an item will be used for current research or only in the longer-term future is impossible to predict.[26]

In reality, further subject breakdowns than humanities, social sciences, sciences and interdisciplinary would likely be needed at least for larger institutions. The other and more problematic requirement for program designation is, of course, that the program costs be realistically and readily quantifiable. Establishing program costs in this fashion is especially difficult for most libraries–except perhaps for the collection development operation, which traditionally divides its materials budget by subject or program. The costs of supporting some of the most important program categories may not be easily identifiable. On the other hand, not only do different subjects or other programmatic categories have different needs and values, they also have different developing research infrastructures, with online uses and capacities evolving at very different rates. These different needs and different access opportunities can at least be reflected in the program budget. We cannot avoid the interdisciplinary category, since the parameters of subjects are notoriously permeable–although like the use of the "administration" category, we must take care not to use the interdisciplinary category as an excuse to avoid difficult categorical budgetary decisions. Tracking and budgeting mediation costs, while difficult, should be within our means. Mediation personnel (presently in reference, collection development and cataloging), for example, frequently have subject specialties. Many paraprofessional staff, on the other hand, such as searchers, reference assistants or copy catalogers, will still need to be included in the interdisciplinary categories.

As in the service budget, it is especially important to include in the program budget "internal" and "external" alternative options. In both the mediation and delivery categories, most of the personnel costs will remain internal and most of the materials costs external–using the definitions established in the service budget. An important part of the program budget process must be to consider how costs can be reduced and/or services enhanced by examining alternatives, as they apply specifically to different institutional programs.

Finally, we will no doubt find in the program budget that administrative costs are even more difficult to integrate than in the service budget–but again, we must not lose sight of the fact that administrative costs are real, and must be accounted for. Including administrative costs provides a clear indication of their effect on program support, requires that they be regularly and routinely justified, and ensures that they will be systematically factored into any budget planning rather than hidden and protected. Such administrative costs might either simply be included in the interdisciplinary column, or some effort might be made to distribute them across institutional programs.

The difficulties and values of such a method as multidimensional budgeting should now be apparent. Like other budgeting methods–although perhaps in a rather simpler fashion–library-wide, multidimensional budgeting would in a sense purchase planning and coordination capabilities somewhat at the expense of clear and easily managed accounting procedures. But such benefits may be worth the costs. A primary drawback of such budgeting methods is the significant expenditure of staff time and energy necessary to quantify and track the expenditures in some of the more important categories. The value added to the budgeting process, however, should be substantial. In the case of multidimensional budgeting, the budget format will force the creation of priorities and encourage the consideration of the full effect of allocation. In the example presented above, in which the same funding is viewed from three different but connected dimensions or perspectives, not only must the first draft of such a budget present all three dimensions, but each change to the initial draft in the review process leading to the final budget also requires adjustments to all three dimensions, providing much more detailed insight into the implications of such adjustments for library services and academic program support. This should enhance significantly the communication and planning value of the deliberation and negotiation process that leads to the final budget draft.

## CONCLUSIONS

If the library must indeed position itself for the gradual but inexorable transition into an age in which information exchange is characterized by the prevalence of online sources, then a major aspect of this work must inevitably be to shift more of the responsibility for scholarly communication to the academy itself. The adverse effect of the practices of commercial science publishers on scholarly information exchange presents only one argument–although certainly a very compelling one–for such action. If the academic library is to participate in–and facilitate–this transformation in scholarly communication, as indeed it should, a more detailed budgeting process, possibly of the multidimensional type suggested above, must be devised and implemented. This redesign will not be without political risk for the library, for to make budgeting a more public process is to invite some controversy. It is, however, only by opening up the budgeting process that the library can successfully inform the community of the true costs of information services, and begin to urge the community to adopt more economically reasonable methods of information transfer. Only through such a public and expanded budgeting process, moreover, can the library demonstrably ensure that it is functioning consciously as the agent of its users–and not in its own interests. And only through such an expanded budgeting process, finally, can the competing traditional jurisdictions within the academic library be somewhat alleviated, and the opportunities for interinstitutional cooperation assessed.

The fundamental rationale for the academic library will remain the same in the online era as it has always been: to provide current and future local users with access to that information they need to do their work in the shortest possible time. In order to continue to achieve that objective in our radically changing technical and economic environment, the library and its institution must consider how to change more of its mediation costs from internal to external, and how to shift more of its delivery costs from external to internal. We need, in other words, for our local users to begin to rely more on mediation services provided (online) by other institutions–in effect, dividing responsibility for specialized subject expertise among institutions. At the same time, more of our delivery costs need to be at least partially internalized by contriving for individual institutions to assume the role of publisher–either of the scholarship of its local faculty or on the basis of some division of subject publication responsibilities across institutions. If this transition is managed gradually and deliberately, moreover, the effect on the availability of library jobs may be minimal: such jobs that are lost by contracting out for mediation might be replaced by the assumption of increased internal responsibilities for delivery.

All such work presupposes, of course, a much closer coordination of responsibilities among institutions than has been practicable in the past. The reasons we have failed to achieve such cooperation are not so much bibliographical or even economic, as they are cultural and political. This failure has been to our disadvantage, and the chronic inability of libraries–and institutions–to form effective alliances will become an increasingly serious impediment to scholarly communication. While economic pressures may force increased coordination among–and within–institutions, and while technical advances may provide improved means for such coordination, each institution must still develop internal techniques that will permit it to overcome those political and cultural obstacles. Since the budgeting activity is by far the most politically driven and culturally revealing process in any institution, it is only reasonable that our work begin there.

## NOTES

1. This is the conclusion of the forthcoming Andrew W. Mellon Foundation report on *University Libraries and Scholarly Communication*. For a preview of that report, see *ARL: A Bimonthly Newsletter of Research Library Issues and Actions* 165 (23 Nov. 1992): 1-2.

2. See Richard Hume Werking, "Allocating the Academic Library's Book Budget: Historical Perspectives and Current Reflections," *The Journal of Academic Librarianship* 14 (July 1988): 140-41.

3. Eugene L. Wiemers, Jr., "Budget," in *Collection Management: A New Treatise*, ed. Charles B. Osburn and Ross Atkinson (Greenwich, Conn.: JAI Press, 1991), Part A: 71.

4. See the remarks by Nancy A. Brown and Jerry Malone on resource control as one base of power in their "The Bases and Uses of Power in a University Library," *Library Administration & Management* 2 (June 1988): 142.

5. Jasper G. Schad, "Fairness in Book Fund Allocation," *College & Research Libraries* 48 (Nov. 1987): 486.

6. G. Stevenson Smith, *Managerial Accounting for Libraries and Other Not-for-Profit Organizations* (Chicago: American Library Association, 1991), 6-7. For a good summary of research on agency theory, see Kathleen M. Eisenhardt, "Agency Theory: An Assessment and Review," *Academy of Management Review* 14 (Jan. 1989): 57-74.

7. See Edwin E. Williams, "Farmington Plan" in *The Encyclopedia of Library and Information Science*, vol. 8 (New York: Dekker, 1972), 361-68.

8. Richard M. Dougherty, "Turning the Serials Crisis to Our Advantage: An Opportunity for Leadership," *Library Administration & Management* 3 (Spring 1989): 60-61.

9. Wiemers, "Budget," p. 73.

10. For a good review of library budgeting, see Michael E.D. Koenig and Deidre C. Stam, "Budgeting and Financial Planning for Libraries," *Advances in Library Administration and Organization* 4 (1985): 77-110.

11. On zero-base budgeting, see Ching-chih Chen, *Zero-Base Budgeting in Library Management: A Manual for Librarians* (Phoenix: Oryx Press, 1980); and more recently, Carol Hodlofski, "Zero-Base Budgeting: A Tool for Cutting Back," *The Bottom Line* 5 (Summer 1991): 13-19. For one of the original accounts of the Planning-Programming-Budget System, from which the goals but also the difficulties of the system are readily apparent, see "Program Planning and Budgeting Theory: Improved Library Effectiveness by Use of the Planning-Programming-Budgeting-System," *Special Libraries* 60 (Sept. 1969): 423-33. See also Michael E.D. Koenig and Victor Alperin, "ZBBB and PPBS: What's Left Now That the Trendiness Has Gone?" *Drexel Library Quarterly* 21 (Summer 1985): 19-38.

12. Collection policies may, of course, as noted in Bonita Bryant, ed., *Guide for Written Collection Policy Statements*, Collection Management and Development guides, No. 3 (Chicago: American Library Association, 1989), p. 3, establish "useful priorities to guide cataloging, retrospective conversion, and preservation decisions," but if the policy does not expressly designate priorities for decision-making outside of collection development, they may well have only a minimal effect on broader library operations.

13. Jeffrey A. Schmidt, "Is It Time to Replace Traditional Budgeting? A Method to Make a Budget More Useful to Management is Proposed," *Journal of Accountancy* 174 (Oct. 1992), 104.

14. Schmidt, p. 104.

15. For current guidelines, see Edward Shreeves, Ed., *Guide to Budget Allocation for Information Resources*, Collection Management and Development Guides, No. 4 (Chicago: American Library Association, 1991), especially section 4.3 on "Structuring the budget."

16. Richard Hume Werking, "Collection Growth and Expenditures in Academic Libraries: A Preliminary Inquiry," *College & Research Libraries* 52 (Jan. 1991), 11-12.

17. This is perhaps one manifestation of "administrative secrecy" as described in Max Weber's classic account of bureaucracy in Part 2, Chapter XI, of his *Economy and Society*.

18. Schmidt does not suggest using the same categories for successive budget dimensions, but this seems to me desirable from a practical perspective in order to map one dimension on to another.

19. See my "The Acquisitions Librarian as Change Agent in the Transition to the Electronic Library," *Library Resources & Technical Services* 36 (Jan. 1992): 7-20.

20. It would also be possible, of course, to further subdivide mediation into such activities as identification and description, and to add a separate subcategory of storage to the category of delivery.

21. On opportunity costs, see Michael Koenig, "Budgets and Budgeting, Part I," *Special Libraries* 68 (July/Aug. 1977): 230-31. More recently, see Dennis P. Carrigan, "Improving Return on Investment: A Proposal for Allocating the Book Budget," *The Journal of Academic Librarianship* 18 (Nov. 1992): 294.

22. Dougherty, "Turning the Serials Crisis," pp. 62-63.

23. If we define "materials" as only those items used by clientele, then we would, of course, need to budget management information as "other."

24. This is admittedly a change to the usual use of the term "program budget," in which budgeting is normally based on agency programs rather than clientele programs. In my example, agency programs are instead the focus of the service budget.

25. For the drawbacks of allocating by academic department, see Jasper G. Schad, "Allocating Materials Budgets in Institutions of Higher Education," *The Journal of Academic Librarianship* 3 (Jan. 1978): 328.

26. In a totally online environment, of course, in which every use is the equivalent of a kind of online circulation transaction, it may be possible at least to track use, and extrapolate expenses on that basis–but whether even the availability of such data would permit the use of such budgeting categories remains doubtful.

# Allocating Library Acquisitions Budgets in an Era of Declining or Static Funding

Judy Webster

## INTRODUCTION

Much has been written in the last half of the twentieth century about the traditional theories and strategies of allocating academic library materials budgets. This paper will provide an overview of the major methods that have evolved in the last 50 years and examine their rationales. Illustrations of the various points made in the paper will involve statistical data gathered from the University of Tennessee Library (see Table 1). An alternate allocation plan will be proposed as a first step to revise former allocation priorities toward more emphasis on user needs. The proposal offers a particularly useful tool when purchasing power declines and all methods of reducing budget allocations seem unattractive.

## OVERVIEW OF TRADITIONAL ALLOCATION METHODS

Academic libraries have experienced phenomenal growth of their collections in the twentieth century. In fact, many have achieved

---

Judy Webster is Head, Acquisitions and Processing Team, University of Tennessee Library, Knoxville, TN.

[Haworth co-indexing entry note]: "Allocating Library Acquisitions Budgets in an Era of Declining or Static Funding." Webster, Judy. Co-published simultaneously in *Journal of Library Administration* (The Haworth Press, Inc.) Vol. 19, No. 2, 1993, pp. 57-74: and: *Declining Acquisitions Budgets: Allocation, Collection Development and Impact Communication* (ed: Sul H. Lee) The Haworth Press, Inc., 1993, pp. 57-74. Multiple copies of this article/chapter may be purchased from The Haworth Document Delivery Center [1-800-3-HAWORTH; 9:00 a.m. - 5:00 p.m. (EST)].

## TABLE 1

### Growth of UTK Library Collection in Volumes

### 1839-1992

| Year | Volumes |
|---|---|
| 1839 | 3,000 |
| 1904 | 20,000 |
| 1923 | 44,904 |
| 1933 | 134,071 |
| 1943 | 230,858 |
| 1953 | 295,891 |
| 1959 | 603,157 |
| 1963 | 642,381 |
| 1968 | 1,000,000* |
| 1973 | 1,125,335 |
| 1983 | 1,421,342 |
| 1992 | 1,959,168** |

Sources:

*Montgomery, James Riley et al., *To Foster Knowledge,* University of Tennessee Press, 1984.

**Association of Research Libraries. *ARL Statistics 1973-1992.*

most of their growth during this period. For example, the University of Tennessee Library, located in Knoxville, held 20,000 volumes in 1904. By 1943, the Library contained 230,858 volumes. Twenty years later its size had tripled to 642,381 volumes. The 1960's brought incredible growth to the institution marked by the celebration of the addition of the one millionth volume to the Library in 1968.[1] From 1963 to 1968, the Library had averaged adding 71,523 volumes per year. In the ten year period between 1963 and 1973 the growth rate averaged 48,295 and from 1973 to 1983, it was 29,600. In the most recent decade from 1983-1992, the growth rate has been approximately 59,758 volumes per year. One hundred seventy-four years elapsed between the founding of the institution until the one millionth volume was purchased, while only 25 years will have been required to reach the second million mark.

The principles of building academic library collections that were developed and widely used in the twentieth century were based upon two largely unchallenged tenets: (1) any library's collection should reflect user needs, and (2) any library's collection should be balanced representing the breadth of the scope of its mission. The central problem of many libraries was deciding what *not to buy*. Librarians have written collection development policies in support of their endeavors to fulfill the twofold mission. A natural tension has developed along the continuum of quality on the one hand and expressed need upon the other. In academic libraries, anticipated use has been one of the most important factors guiding the selection of library materials. In times of fiscal abundance, the terms *block buying* and the *acquisitions vacuum cleaner* were used to describe useful practices of acquiring a large number of volumes in a relatively short period of time. Blanket order plans and eventually approval plans evolved as additional broad collecting methods.[2]

The means of allocation usually employed to insure the timely expenditure of these burgeoning library budgets were one or more of the following: historical, zero-based, formulas, ranking, and percentages. In the historical method, allocations are based upon previous year's expenditures. Local institutional politics may affect the allocation of funds with the more vocal and influential faculty receiving a larger allocation for their particular subject areas. The previous year's expenditures are usually taken as a base against which additional funds are applied. In the use of the zero-based method the division of resources requires an annual reconsideration and recalculation of budget categories against selected criteria. This method is ostensibly more flexible and subject to change because it does not consider the previous year's expenditures. Allocation formulas apply weighted variables equitably according to the criteria selected by the individual library. Ranking is a variation of the formula method. It also involves the application of weighted criteria to the various budget categories, but the number of criteria may vary from category to category. Numerical values are assigned to the criteria, and then the values are totaled by budget category. The totals are assigned a rank order with the units of a higher rank receiving larger allocations. A percentage based method applies the same percentage of the total institutional budget each allocated unit receives to the library materials budget. It assumes allocation units correspond to the overall institutional budget categories.[3]

Various methods of further apportioning the library materials budget have also been used. Division by department, location, method of purchase, format, and by subject are some common ways to further subdivide the entire acquisitions budget.[4]

Most of the allocation literature refers to various versions of the formulaic approach. A brief review of the historical development of the allocation formulas provides an overview of the rationales that have been incorporated into this process through the years. Allocation using highly structured formulas has achieved some degree of popularity, but according to a fairly recent survey, the use of formulas in academic libraries has declined from a high of 73% in the 1940's to 40% in 1989.[5]

There are two excellent recent articles that summarize the history and use of allocation formulas. One, published in *JAL* in 1988, was written by Donna Packer and the other by John M. Budd was published in *LAPT* in 1991. According to Budd, the first effort in formulating an allocation scheme may have been made by William Randall writing in 1931. Randall used average price per title (by department) and the number of books published in those subject areas per year. An important qualification was noted by the author. Apparently, he believed that his own allocation scheme could be effective "only if the book budget is large enough to care for the needs of the library."[6]

Over the next 40 years many formulas with different variables were postulated. Gradually, a standard list of potential variables available to be included in an allocation formula were developed.[7] By 1973, according to Greaves, the most frequently used elements were the number of faculty, enrollment of students by level, amount of research generated, cost of materials, collection adequacy, number of courses offered, circulation statistics, past expenditure record. Several authors also advocated that various measures of the use of library materials be incorporated into the formulas. Budd concludes that the one constant in all of the literature on the use of formulas in academic libraries is that no one formula will suit all circumstances.[8]

The reasons for using formulas need only a quick review for our purposes. All formulas attempt to quantify the allocation of resources according to an established rationale applied using weighted variables that are applied equitably to certain subdivisions of the library materials budget. The basis, according to Schad, is to allocate by subject area according to the size of the department's contribution to the academic institution. Apparently, formulas have been used as an effective means of solving political dilemmas of inequitable resource allocations. A recent (March, 1992) article, by Charles Lowry proposed another new version of a formula which the author terms a matrix. I would like to call your attention to his concluding sentences which I will quote:

> However, in the end the matrix formula cannot overcome the central problem of budgeting–insufficient funds. Any formula may satisfy acquisition needs if sufficient funds are put into it. *No formula will overcome inadequate funding.*[9]

The University of Tennessee Library has generally used the historical precedence method of allocating the acquisitions budget. The allocation of the entire materials budget was sub-divided into four broad categories: periodicals, serials, approval plans, and firm orders. The firm order portion of the budget was further subdivided by branch libraries, central reference, and academic subject areas corresponding, for the most part, to academic budgeting entities recognized by the University. There have been challenges to that method from time to time, but as of this writing a very informal allocation process is still being used with the allocations generally being controlled by the collection development librarian. Serious challenges to this approach have never materialized from any constituency. Last year the process was expanded to include a committee of selector-librarians who suggested specific allocation amounts. The committee used some of the traditional formulaic variables and has applied them informally to adjust the allocation amounts upward or downward to reflect changes in programs and curriculum. This variation in method did elicit some controversy, because a few funds, heretofore thought to be inviolate, were decreased substantially.

## *THE DILEMMA*

Will these methods which were derived in years of overall institutional growth continue to serve us well into the next century? There have been signs at the University of Tennessee Library that years of growth will not continue and that we must face a future of continued erosion of our purchasing power. Our ARL statistics for the past two years illustrate the present situation (see Table 2). The best we may be able to hope for is to retain our overall percentage of the institutional budget. We are not simply facing a difficult time that will pass in a year or two. Therefore, we should begin viewing the present situation as the way the future will be.

How then, can we possibly continue to fulfill our twofold mission? If we find any truth in the assertions that formulas only work well when there is adequate funding, what strategies will we be able to employ as competition for scarce dollars increases among disciplines and the interdisciplinary nature of research continues to proliferate? When funds are inadequate to achieve our goals, we must revisit our two-fold mission and establish priorities between the two goals. In addition to building balanced collections for potential use, research libraries are being called upon to be even more responsive to the immediate needs of users than they have in the past. Frequently, funds are not adequate to purchase everything identified by traditional selection means.[10] When the choice must be made between

## TABLE 2

## UTK LIBRARY
## ARL STATISTICS
## 1990/91-1991/92

| Category | 1990/91 | Rank | 1991/92 | Rank |
|---|---|---|---|---|
| Volumes held | 1,914,674 | 77 | 1,959,168 | 76 |
| Volumes added | 46,101 | 94 | 49,630 | 85 |
| Current serials | 22,972 | 50 | 18,269 | 75 |
| Materials expend. | 3,635,202 | 70 | 3,647,796 | 81 |
| Total expend. | 9,113,296 | 79 | 9,054,728 | 88 |
| Serial expend. | 2,591,139 | 51 | 2,388,081 | 71 |
| ILL-Items lent | 15,529 | 72 | 19,433 | 62 |
| ILL-Items borrowed | 13,042 | 36 | 13,765 | 36 |

collecting for a future need and collecting for an evident present one, which one should we favor?

Although use statistics have been one of the variables considered in formulas for many years, we advocate the integration of use statistics into collection development planning in a unique way–not as a single variable among many, but as a specific guide to fulfilling a library's mission. In the future, librarians should openly acknowledge the fact that evidence of use by subject will be considered an important factor in the decision to purchase and retain a physical item rather than simply provide access. In order to more clearly illustrate how use statistics gathered by subject could be important in future allocation plans, I will briefly describe the research project that I and my colleague, William Britten, undertook using data from the UTK Library online system. Throughout our study, we have understood the circulation of a physical item to be *evidence of interest in the specific subject of the item checked out*. We have not dealt with questions of the quality or ultimate usefulness of specific titles in this project.

## *THE STUDY*

At the University of Tennessee Library, the automated tracking of circulating items began in 1982 with the implementation of our circulation module. The statistics remained largely unused until December of 1990 when we began a new research project. The purpose of the study was to analyze the MARC records of highly circulated titles in each Library of Congress class to discover if patterns of commonality existed among high-use titles. Our hypothesis was that there would be common characteristics among these titles and that library selectors would be able to use the data as a component in their future selection work.

The portion of the collection used in the study was comprised of monographic items that held the highest cumulative circulation counts on the automated system (circulation data for periodicals is incomplete on the UTK automated system). After eliminating all but the monographic titles, there remained just less than one million items, which were first sorted by call number to group the LC classes. Sorting by class allowed the data to be gathered that would be useful to subject bibliographers. Then the items were sorted in descending order by the total number of times circulated on the online system from 1982 through 1990. The result was a ranking of all titles in each LC class from most circulated to least circulated.

The next step was to select portions of the collection to examine. Since the plan was to inspect each title, it was decided that the study would be confined to the top 400 circulating titles of LC classes with at least 10,000 items. A group of 20 LC classes resulted, which represented large segments of the collection where significant amounts of money were spent and bibliographers had much selection work to do. Choosing to select the top 400 titles in each of these 20 groups was an arbitrary decision for the purposes of limiting the study to a manageable size, but it allowed investigation of the cream of the crop–titles which ranged in number of circulations from a high of 161 for a title in the class LB to a "low" of 8 circulations for a title in class D. These 8,000 titles (20 groups of 400) averaged over 26 circulations each (the average circulation rate for all 921,596 monographic items in the collection is 2.65 circulations per item).

Comparing the MARC records of thousands of titles for indications of commonality was potentially labor intensive and intimidating. The library's integrated system, however, allowed extracting specific MARC tags from the online catalog database for the records gathered in the circulation database. Utilizing this technique it was possible, for example, to capture all of the subject headings, all of the authors, or all of the dates of publication for any of the groups of 400 highly used titles. These groups of MARC tags were then sorted to allow easy visual inspection to spot the clusters of commonality that characterize popular titles.

The 20 groups of 400 popular titles were first analyzed for frequency of subject heading occurrence (see Table 3). The data set was next analyzed for imprint dates (see Table 4).

Given that the data represents circulations recorded from 1982 to 1990, indications are that titles remain well used for many years after their publication, even outside the areas where this might be expected. It appears that for the UTK Libraries' monograph collection, the hard sciences are less currency oriented than many of the social sciences.

Analyzing the occurrence of authors among the top items in each class proved to be useful only in the literature classes of the study—PQ, PR, PS, and PT. Among the nonfiction classes there was almost no commonality related to authors, and, when an author did appear several times in the top 400 list it was nearly always due to the library's owning multiple copies of one title. However, studying the occurrence of authors in literature allowed a comparison between the use of criticism versus the use of original work (see Table 5).

Lastly, the language indicator in MARC field 008 was analyzed for LC classes PQ and PT. It was of considerable interest to us that the most highly used titles in PT are in English. A relatively small percentage of Spanish titles in PQ accounts for a fairly high number of the high use items. We also evaluated the circulation rates for all titles in the two classes, PQ and PT, as well as PL and PG, two

## TABLE 3

### Occurrences of Subject Headings
### From the 400 Most-circulated Books for Selected LC Classes

| | | |
|---|---|---|
| BF | Nonverbal Communication | 39 |
| BF | Stress | 37 |
| BF | Cognition | 21 |
| BF | Dreams | 20 |
| BF | Psychoanalysis | 16 |
| BF | Attitude | 14 |
| BF | Witchcraft | 14 |
| BF | Anxiety | 11 |
| BF | Interpersonal Relations | 9 |
| BF | Control | 8 |
| | | |
| HV | Child Abuse | 51 |
| HV | Capital Punishment | 50 |
| HV | Suicide | 36 |
| HV | Alcoholics/Alcoholism | 27 |
| HV | Rape | 23 |
| HV | Sign Language/Deaf, Means of Communication | 19 |
| HV | Animals, Treatment of | 18 |
| HV | Wife Abuse | 17 |
| HV | Children, Deaf | 15 |
| HV | Deaf, Education | 12 |
| | | |
| RC | Anorexia Nervosa/Bulimarexia | 45 |
| RC | Family Psychotherapy | 27 |
| RC | AIDS | 24 |
| RC | Depression, Mental | 22 |
| RC | Psychotherapy | 21 |
| RC | Schizophrenia | 19 |
| RC | Rational-emotive Psychotherapy | 17 |
| RC | Psychoanalysis | 14 |
| RC | Obesity | 12 |
| RC | Alcoholism | 11 |

| | | |
|---|---|---|
| PS | Frost, Robert | 48 |
| PS | Miller, Arthur | 30 |
| PS | O'Connor, Flannery | 28 |
| PS | Williams, Tennessee | 27 |
| PS | Hawthorne, Nathaniel | 24 |
| PS | Poe, Edgar Allen | 23 |
| PS | Plath, Sylvia | 16 |
| PS | Hemmingway, Ernest | 10 |
| PS | Dickinson, Emily | 8 |
| PS | Hughes, Langston | 8 |
| PT | Ibsen, Henrik | 108 |
| PT | Kafka, Franz | 40 |
| PT | Goethe | 15 |
| PT | Strindberg, August | 14 |
| PT | Brecht, Bertold | 12 |
| PT | German Literature - 18th Century | 6 |
| PT | Dramatists - Norwegian - Biography | 5 |
| PT | Publishers and publishing - Germany | 4 |
| PT | Cotta, Johan | 4 |
| PT | Marat, Jean Paul | 4 |

classes that were not in the overall study. Even though circulation rates are often dismal, research libraries cannot cease buying foreign language titles. To ensure a higher probability of buying useful items, however, the methodology presented in this study could be applied separately to the top-circulating foreign titles to determine their common characteristics.

As an additional step in our study, we searched the online catalogs of other research libraries for several of the most highly circulated subject headings to assess the comparative strength of our collection. Three peer libraries were chosen using these criteria: similarity of collection size, ability to perform keyword searches in the online catalog, and remote Internet accessibility. Since the UTK collection is fully converted to machine-readable records, items located in peer online catalogs but not found in the UTK online catalog would be potential candidates for collecting at UTK.

## TABLE 4

### Distribution of Imprint Dates
### From the 400 Most-circulated Books for Selected LC Classes

|     | pre-1960 | 1960's | 1970's | 1980's |
|-----|----------|--------|--------|--------|
| B   | 78       | 116    | 127    | 78     |
| BF  | 24       | 52     | 198    | 126    |
| D   | 58       | 105    | 129    | 106    |
| DA  | 86       | 80     | 143    | 89     |
| DS  | 85       | 126    | 136    | 50     |
| E   | 44       | 102    | 158    | 96     |
| F   | 86       | 79     | 114    | 120    |
| HC  | 19       | 58     | 141    | 182    |
| HD  | 18       | 15     | 110    | 256    |
| HF  | 18       | 44     | 173    | 165    |
| HV  | 10       | 37     | 166    | 186    |
| LB  | 10       | 47     | 181    | 162    |
| PN  | 53       | 88     | 121    | 137    |
| PQ  | 85       | 126    | 136    | 50     |
| PR  | 65       | 154    | 116    | 63     |
| PS  | 30       | 132    | 160    | 77     |
| PT  | 86       | 132    | 119    | 56     |
| QA  | 16       | 60     | 137    | 187    |
| QC  | 44       | 101    | 136    | 119    |
| RC  | 7        | 23     | 128    | 241    |

A tool such as the OCLC/Amigos Collection Analysis System on CD-ROM could be used as an alternative to comparisons made from searching remote online catalogs.

At this point the study suggested several areas for follow-up activity. The data uncovered many subject headings that were extremely popular, as indicated by high circulation levels. But were these topics consistently popular over time or had they been hot topics for a year or two? The answer to this question would be important when deciding to add titles to the collection. Since the online system does retain the details of circulation transactions, date due slips of books were examined in the stacks for three of the highly circulating subjects.

Another follow-up activity for subjects that appear to be overbur-

## TABLE 5

Distribution of Books about an Author vs. Books by an Author
From the 400 Most-circulated Books for Selected LC Classes

| LC Class | Author | Books about | Books by |
|---|---|---|---|
| PQ | Samuel Beckett | 7 | 15 |
| PQ | Albert Camus | 24 | 11 |
| PQ | Moliere | 18 | 12 |
| PQ | Jean Paul Sartre | 5 | 10 |
| PR | William Shakespeare | 46 | 15 |
| PR | Geoffrey Chaucer | 19 | 9 |
| PS | Robert Frost | 48 | 7 |
| PS | Steven King | 0 | 7 |
| PS | Arthur Miller | 30 | 2 |
| PS | Sylvia Plath | 16 | 8 |
| PT | Goethe | 15 | 22 |
| PT | Henrik Ibsen | 108 | 34 |
| PT | Franz Kafka | 46 | 8 |

dened is an analysis of titles collected by peer libraries. Aside from simply adding these titles to our collection, if that were possible, we attempted to determine what selection strategies would be likely to locate such titles in the future. For example, among the popular titles in BF held by the 3 peer libraries, it was noted that several were from one publisher (this same publisher showed up in interlibrary loan borrowing reports), several were published in Britain, and several were numbered series. Obtaining the publisher's catalog, locating more British sources, and placing the series on standing order would be ways to ensure higher levels of future collection in these subject areas.

LC class QC (Physics) was one of the 20 classes included in the study. The distribution of imprint dates showed that a relatively high number of the top circulating books were published prior to 1970. Because currency of information is assumed to be of importance for science titles, further investigation was done. Of the top 400 circulating books in QC, 51 of them have the subject heading *quantum theory*. Looking at the full records of these 51 books, it was noted that the majority of them were basic texts, as evidenced by titles beginning *Introduction to . . ., Elementary Quantum . . .,* and *Principles of. . . .* Also, the majority were older texts. These facts prompted a follow-up extract of all books in QC with the subject heading *quantum theory,* which indicated that all basic titles on quantum theory are very much in demand, but the collection does not contain many recent publications. Again, Internet searching of peer library catalogs was used to located candidates to fill the gap.

The methodology of this study is a valid means of assessing trends of demand for specific types of items in a library's collection, for uncovering areas that have been under collected and are overburdened with use, and for exposing areas that have been well collected but rarely circulate. As part of an overall collection management program, the data should be interpreted within the context of the user environment–the curriculum, faculty research interests, etc. Analyzing periods of shorter duration would establish the staying power of popular subjects, resolving the problem of checking date due slips.

The method presented here also provides practical techniques that can be replicated in libraries with automated systems. The methodology rests on the ability to create a database of MARC records sorted by call number and including circulation counts. Once this is done, subsequent abstracts of subject headings, authors, imprint dates, etc., for a portion of the collection are easily obtained. An LC class can be quickly analyzed at the request of a selector.

Would libraries following this methodology be sacrificing a collection broadly representative of all publications in all subjects? Yes, this method advocates giving precedence to items in categories of known popularity over those which have attracted little use over time. Would the collection eventually stagnate as users are offered only items which had been used before? No, our method is meant to be a component of an overall collection development plan that would also include traditional methods of selection–it is the emphasis that is shifting. If all libraries adopted the practice of comparing holdings, would that foster homogenization, with all collections tending toward a similar core? Not at all! Following this methodology would lead to a collection that reflects user demand, which in turn reflects the unique characteristics of each library's constituency.[11]

A library should not focus completely on specific subject headings because there may be generalized low-level use throughout many disciplines. One of the general time-honored collecting principles has been that, by the physical collection of books together in a physical space in a library, research and the general advancement of knowledge would be facilitated. In this circumstance, there should be evidence of broad-based use, and libraries should retain financial support for balancing the collection. A comparison of two LC classes from the UTK study will further illustrate this point (see Table 6).

The class BF contains 12,831 monographic items with an average of 6.35 circulations per item. The entire class is an active one with 77% of the items circulating at least once during the period of the study. The class PT has 24,603 monographic items with an average of only .69 circulations per item. Only 22% of the items have circulated at least once in ten years. The high percentage of circulations in the class BF indicates that the discipline is one with broad-based use. We would not only want to purchase future titles of the highest circulating status but we would definitely want to continue to collect broadly. Conversely, PT is very narrow in its range of use. For this class and others like it, a more narrowly focused plan of collecting based more upon the high use subjects is indicated.

By collecting for anticipated demand based on actual evidence of interest in specific subjects and minimizing the purchase of items known to circulate infrequently, libraries will be able to satisfy user demands in spite of shrinking budgets. Along with other collection-use statistics, the reports presented in this study represent the tools of the trade for demand-driven collection development in an automated environment.

Libraries may find that using the methodology of identifying

## TABLE 6
## Comparing Two Classes

**BF (Psychology)**

12,831 monographic items
6.35 average circulations per item
77% of items have circulated at least once on OLIS

- Most popular subject: Nonverbal Communication.
- Of the top 25 circulating items, 10 are about Nonverbal Communication.
- There are 77 items in BF with the subject heading Nonverbal Communication; 76 of these items have circulated (99%), with an average of 24 circulations per item.

**PT (Germanic Literatures)**

24,603 monographic items
.69 average circulations per item
22% of the items have circulated at least once on OLIS

- Items about or by Henrik Ibsen (173 titles) account for 18% of all PT circulations; these 173 titles have a circulation rate of 11.2, with 89% of them circulating at least once.
- Of the top 25 circulating PT items, 21 are Ibsen-related.
- Second-most popular are items about or by Strindberg. There are 119 Strindberg-related titles, with a circs/item rate of 4.59. 69% of these titles have circulated, and they account for 4.5% of PT circulations.
- Third-most popular are items about or by Kafka. There are 295 Kafka-related titles, with a circs/item rate of 2.4. 55% of the Kafka items have circulated, accounting for 6% of PT circulations.
- Together, items about or by Ibsen, Strindberg, and Kafka comprise 2.6% of the PT collection, but they account for 28.6% of circulations.

both the subject areas of high use and ones with low use will inform their allocation process in a better, more current, forward-looking way. To maximize effectiveness, however, libraries should identify their "high use" subject headings on an annual basis, assign them as collecting areas to specific selectors, and allocate a portion of the budget to fund the acquisition of identified materials. Phasing in this procedure over time will make the transition easier.

A specific fund devoted to the purchase of high-use subjects could be created. It would be a fund under the central administration of the library. Requests from the assigned selectors or from anyone would be purchased from this fund rather than the normal subject/departmental firm order allocation providing an incentive for the identification of materials in the high-use subject areas and freeing up funds for other purchases to further balance the library's collection. Collecting in this manner is neutral toward academic funding units. It does not matter who is using the materials; it only matters that someone is.

In the future, allocation methods will probably continue to be differentiated by the types of payments required, i.e., one-time orders, subscriptions and standing orders for reasons of fiscal control. While the methodology described above related to monographs only, the use of periodicals and serials will also require scrutiny. Use studies will also be essential for the other categories of library materials. Reviews of subscriptions and standing orders will need to be done on an annual basis. Libraries will have to become much more flexible in their ability to cancel, reinstate and order new titles that require a continuing commitment. We will not be able to begin each year's budgeting cycle with the assumption of a certain level of expenditure in any of these categories. Our ability to prove use of these valuable and increasingly expensive materials is also imperative. Selectors will need to know how many of their current subscriptions are actually being used on an annual basis. The goal would be to calculate the proportion of the total allocation in any subject area that would be funding actual use versus potential use.

I also advocate finding ways to move away from the traditional allocation by academic department or subject area toward larger groupings of subject areas, perhaps the humanities, social sciences, and the sciences in addition to creating or increasing an interdisciplinary and general purpose use fund to support the total collection. Access services, including document delivery should also be included as standard budget categories. Additional study needs to be given to many of the ideas represented here, but we must begin creating new ways to apportion our library materials budgets that maximize our flexibility and insure our ability to respond to immediate user needs.

## REFERENCES

1. James Riley et al., *To Foster Knowledge* (University of Tennessee Press, 1984) pp. 36, 160, 275.
2. Mary Duncan Carter and Wallace John Bonk *Building Library Collections* (Scarecrow Press, 1969) pp. 44-52.
3. Edward Shreeves, ed., *Guide to Budget Allocation for Information Resources* (Chicago: American Library Association, 1991), pp. 9-11.
4. Rose Mary Magrill and John Corbin *Acquisition Management and Collection Development in Libraries* (American Library Association, 1989) pp. 56-57.
5. John M. Budd and Kay Adams, "Allocation Formulas in Practice," *Library Acquisitions: Practice and Theory* 13:381-390 (1989).
6. John M. Budd, "Allocation Formulas in the Literature: A Review," *Library Acquisitions: Practice and Theory* 15:95-107 (1991).
7. Donna Packer, "Acquisitions Allocations: Equity, Politics, and Formulas," *Journal of Academic Librarianship* 14: 276-286 (November, 1988).
8. Budd, "Allocation Formulas in the Literature: A Review," pp. 98-99.
9. Charles B. Lowry, "Reconciling Pragmatism, Equity, and Need in the Formula Allocation of Book and Serial Funds" *College and Research Libraries* 53:121-137(March, 1992).
10. Mark Cyzyk, "Canon Formation, Library Collections, and the Dilemma of Collection Development." *College & Research Libraries* 54:58-65.
11. William A. Britten and Judith D. Webster, "Comparing Characteristics of Highly Circulated Titles for Demand-Driven Collection Development" *College and Research Libraries* 53:239-248 (May, 1992).

# Justifying Collection Budgets: Indexing Materials Costs

Gay N. Dannelly

The costs of library materials have soared over the past several years. Between inflation, currency fluctuations, and the development of new formats for information identification and retrieval, libraries and their home institutions have been sorely tested trying to maintain current programs, much less support new programs or initiatives. The need for a new budgeting approach, agreed to by all parties participating in the budget allocation process, is underscored by the findings of the recently published Mellon Study on *University Libraries and Scholarly Communication.* The study found that "When we compare increases in the average price of hardcover books and the average price of periodicals subscriptions, we find that between 1963 and 1970 the respective price indexes increased by comparable rates. Over these seven years the prices of these types of publications also increased roughly in line with the overall price index for all goods and services." The report continues, "Beginning in 1970, however, the pattern changed profoundly. While the price of books continued to increase at about the same rate as the GNP . . . until about 1978, the price index for periodicals began to increase much more rapidly and to diverge sharply from the index for books and the overall index. This was precisely the

---

Gay N. Dannelly is Collection Development Officer, The Ohio State University Libraries, Columbus, OH.

[Haworth co-indexing entry note]: "Justifying Collection Budgets: Indexing Materials Costs." Dannelly, Gay N. Co-published simultaneously in *Journal of Library Administration* (The Haworth Press, Inc.) Vol. 19, No. 2, 1993, pp. 75-88: and: *Declining Acquisitions Budgets: Allocation, Collection Development and Impact Communication* (ed: Sul H. Lee) The Haworth Press, Inc., 1993, pp. 75-88. Multiple copies of this article/chapter may be purchased from The Haworth Document Delivery Center [1-800-3-HAWORTH; 9:00 a.m. - 5:00 p.m. (EST)].

© 1993 by The Haworth Press, Inc. All rights reserved.

decade when a great many new journals were founded, and there are reasons to believe that the proliferation of specialized journals had a marked effect on the prices of periodicals."[1] Additional confirmation of this cost pattern was provided by the Association of Research Libraries in March 1993. ARL reported that based on members' reported expenditure data during the 1982-1992 decade non-serial materials increased at a rate of slightly over 30 percent in contrast to serials which increased at a rate 67% higher than the CPI.[2]

When considering funding justification methodologies or processes it is important to consider the environmental and cultural issues that are an integral part of any budget and planning program. It is not only libraries that face economic hard times. Our institutions and communities are facing them too. As Carolyn Bucknall has noted, "Our institutional woes have roots in national economic policy that we, as librarians, cannot eradicate."[3] Economic, political and social realties impact our budgets and the best we can do is to cope creatively and to develop strategies to deal with decreasing funding for traditional library activities, spiraling demands for both traditional and electronic information, and a technological brave new world that is turning not only our profession, but our society upside down.

Within the university, and it seems clear that this holds true for many if not all governing bodies of libraries, we are dealing with a traditional bureaucracy that is in the process of transforming itself. It is coping with declining resources, increasing demands from faculty and students, external pressures from funding and governing bodies, and a technological revolution that must be an integral part of the educational setting in order to maintain institutional credibility in the employment market, a particularly strategic concern for state assisted institutions.

Tom Shaughnessy includes among the university's pressures the "projected decline–up until 1995–in the college age population and the demands for support of other campus agencies–computing centers, laboratories, recruitment and retention programs, assessment programs, etc. The fact is that library finance is not determined by academic need any more than higher education finance is determined by institutional need."[4]

As the competition for scarce resources escalates, the budgeting process continues to become more complex and competitive within the university. Robert Munn, in "The Bottomless Pit, or the Academic Library as Viewed from the Administration Building," wrote "... the conventional wisdom is simply no longer useful in the area of resource allocation. It does not help the Administration determine whether..." additional funds "would be better spent on books or on the addition of new staff in the department of civil engineering. At the moment, neither do the analytical techniques developed by institutional research.... Since nobody yet appears to have the slightest idea how to make a cost benefit analysis of the contribution of the library, few administrators feel justified in straying far from the traditional percentage."[5] While this is no longer the case, in terms of percentage allocations, unless a rapid and continuing DECREASE in the percentage of general education funds allocated to the library is included, it is important to recognize the need for objective external evidence that supports library budget proposals.

Munn goes on to say, "The current pressure to introduce modern management practices into the universities will not leave libraries unaffected. Such techniques as program budgeting require a much more rigorous analysis of the balance of return against investment than has ever been applied to libraries.... similar questions are certain to be asked. It might be prudent for academic librarians to have some answers."[6] Even for those administrators who consider the library of central importance to the university's mission the current cost crisis and the need for electronic resources has exacerbated the situation and made it extremely difficulty for the library and the university to cope with budgeting and does indeed, make the library appear to be a "bottomless pit."

Among other conditions that have direct impact on the cost problems faced by libraries, John Berry has identified the "marketplace" and technology that serves the marketplace as the two biggest issues facing libraries today.[3] The concept of information as a saleable commodity strikes at the heart of our professional values. While librarians seek to provide the maximum information to our public, we also try to acquire it at minimal cost to our libraries, and to provide it at no cost to our users. The rapidly increasing costs of materials in general, and serials in particular, is aggravated by the fact that electronic information is not only expensive, but is often limited by site licensing restrictions. The convergence of these trends is not only a major frustration, but places direct limits on the resources that can be made available to library users.

Moore and Schauder have predicted that "Library funding–both in academic and public libraries–is the issue of the decade and will probably be the issue which consumes the energy of library managers to the end of this century."[8] The literature on the causes of the library fiscal crises is broad. But there are common themes that run through much of the discussion of the present situation. These include:

1. Increasing numbers of researchers.[9]
2. Increasing pressure to publish for tenure and promotion
3. Increase in size and number of journals
4. Increase in scholarly publication
5. Changing undergraduate curriculums that require more use of library resources.
6. Inflation
7. Changing value of the dollar
8. Technology and its impact on collection resources

The latter item is particularly difficult. Many of the electronic resources acquired by libraries duplicate the contents of paper resources already owned by the library but provide new and more efficient access to the information. Now, instead of acquiring duplicate copies of journals, libraries are duplicating indexes and abstracts, statistical resources and similar materials; and often don't own them but only lease them.

Universities and others have coped with budget crises in two primary ways: direct decrease of the allocation for library materials budgets, decreasing library budget purchasing power by providing no increases; and assisting libraries to minimally maintain current purchasing power.

Perhaps the most notable recent example of attempting to maintain purchasing power is found at the University of Toronto. The University has supported the Libraries by agreeing to compensate for fluctuations in currency, a particularly difficult problem in Canada. This has worked for several years, but is now being phased out.[10]

From the 1970's to at least the mid-1980's Harvard University's Widener Library indexed their periodical prices, primarily using local data and correlating the results with national indexes. They were dependent on using published data and the window between the availability of data and the submission date for budget proposals was a continuing source of disquiet. Indexing was apparently not applied to the remainder of the materials budget.[11] There are undoubtedly other examples of such funding models, but they are few and far between. Even in the most orderly institutions, library materials funding has usually been viewed in an opportunistic and year-by-year process.

It is clear in reviewing available cost data that library materials costs, in general, increase at a rate higher than the standard Consumer Price Index. The current crises in funding makes it obvious that not only budget levels but budget processes have usually failed to take adequate account of library costs above the consumer price index levels. In order to cope with rising costs and the continuing justification of funding needs, The Ohio State University has developed a somewhat different approach to library materials funding.

The Ohio State University Libraries participates in the University's annual budget review process. At the budget review held in April 1988, the University's Vice-President for Finance requested the University Libraries, in cooperation with the Health Sciences and Law Libraries, and with the participation of staff from the Office of Financial Management, to develop a library materials index. His hope was that such a tool would assist the University budget process and provide a consistent source for measuring library materials expenditures against the marketplace.

In many ways the political and educational process was as important as the development of the index itself. Initially, the academic administration was clearly distrustful of the libraries' documentation. And they were clearly tired of the litany of materials budget woes reported to them. However, following the initial nine months of education and negotiation the Provost had been convinced of the legitimacy of our needs. In addition, the fiscal and budget planning staffs became much more knowledgeable and are fully committed to the process.

To describe the evolution of the Index, it is important to understand what an index is. Based on our experience, it is important to understand the term in the same way that accountants and financial planners use the term. An index is a tool for comparing the cost of the same item or items over time. The components of an index are frequently described as the index marketbasket. For example, an index tracks the cost of coal, gas and electricity in an energy marketbasket or the wages of an administrative assistant 1, a secretary and a mail room supervisor in a staff marketbasket; categories or components that stay the same although the costs change.

In the case of libraries, our indexes track similar kinds of materials. Thus the North American Academic Books index tracks the market based on monograph titles supplied by major approval vendors during a specific year. While the titles are not the same, the nature of the materials is relatively constant. The serial indexes track either the same or comparable titles over time, as does the *Choice* Academic Books Index. The foreign indexes, so well explained by Fred Lynden on a number of occasions, provide much the same kind of information.

There are several issues that must be considered when developing an index proposal to be used by the institution rather than the library. First is the question of who is to be included. At a large institution, there may be several libraries not only physically outside of the "main library" but also reporting to other administrative units such as the Law School or the Medical College. The OSU administration had traditionally applied the same increase figure to the materials budgets for all three library systems. This, of course, left all of us underfunded. In order to provide equivalent budget support mechanisms, the University administration directed that the three systems, University, Health Sciences and Law Libraries, all participate in the project.

All three libraries agreed. After much discussion and documentation, the administration also agreed that each library system could have a separate index and that budgets would be adjusted differentially based on the specific index. Thus a general university guideline figure with suballocations for the Health Sciences, Law and

University Libraries. Each has its' own index figures, composed of the same four elements, but adjusted by the differing increases or decreases in the discipline areas.

The second issue is to define what is to be included in the index. In our case the university allocation for library materials also included binding. Due to the difference in inflation rates and the comparative dearth of timely information on binding costs, it was agreed to move the binding budget to an operating budget line.

A third issue is to determine the time frame in which the budget must be proposed. This is particularly strategic for two reasons. First, it doesn't matter how good the arguments are and how persuasive the presentation is at a budget hearing, if the money has already been preliminarily allocated elsewhere. OSU traditionally held annual budget hearings for every college and major program from February until early May. What most deans and program directors apparently did not realize was that the preliminary allocations were done in January and February and that the hearings had relatively little impact on the coming fiscal year, but were rather a status review and projection for the next year; i.e., two years ahead. Naturally there were more timely adjustments, but the allocation process and the hearing process were not directly related for the coming fiscal year.

Secondly, it is important to seek external information, if that is required, on a timely basis. Otherwise, an index can be two years out of date at the time it is initially applied and will not provide the continuing maintenance of purchasing power that it was designed to accomplish.

The fourth issue is to develop an index that is based on appropriately specific or general information. If it is generated solely from internal data then you have greater flexibility in defining the categories that should be indexed, assuming that your data exists and does not require an excessive amount of manipulation to become useful. Using external data has other complications.

The most widely recognized index of higher education costs is the *Higher Education Price Index*[12] published annually by Research Associates. When the Ohio State project began the HEPI index was considered to be an adequate methodology but a totally inappropriate distribution of costs across categories of materials, source data, and reflection of currency fluctuations.

Following detailed discussions including Financial Management and the administrations of all three libraries it was agreed that four primary categories of library materials would serve as the basis for the "Library Materials Index." These categories were domestic books and serials and foreign books and serials. This model followed the HEPI format. The "Index," however, differed from HEPI in the distribution of expenditures across these categories and in the sources of data used to document price changes.

The Libraries initially suggested that data produced by our acquisition system, Innovacq, would be the most appropriate source of such data since it so accurately reflects our institutional library experience. Financial Management strongly preferred data from an objective external source and required that we identify and use such data. In trying to do so the biggest hurdle was to identify data that was appropriate for all three library systems. University Libraries and the Health Sciences Library were relatively clear, but data for Law libraries is available only on a very delayed basis which defeats the purpose of an index for maintaining current purchasing power. Following a rigorous review of available cost data it was agreed that medical data would be used for the law library serials costs since it closely reflected the price fluctuations in legal literature. And it was the only available alternative in three of the four categories.

Three sources of cost data, produced on an annual basis, and available by January of each year were identified. Domestic books costs were represented by the "North American Academic Books Index."[13] This index tracks costs of materials supplied on domestic approval plans and provides broad subject categories that allow the specific identification of medical and legal literature.

Foreign books were represented by the Library of Congress foreign book costs index.[14] This source was selected as the broadest representation of foreign pricing information, despite the vagaries of acquisition and selection decisions it reflected. Other foreign data was available only on a very delayed basis and for very few countries. While OSU's primary foreign expenditures remain in Western Europe, an increasing percentage of acquisition activity occurs in other areas and only the Library of Congress was able to provide adequate current data.

Serial data is provided by the Faxon Company in a special annual report prepared at the end of the subscription payment year.[15] This report does not provide the average cost of serials, but is based rather on the Faxon weighted average data which includes only those titles actually paid for in a specific year and received by four or more customers in either their academic or medical markets. This provides a realistic measure of actual expenditures rather than an estimate of costs across all titles that may include those that are inactive or that have ceased without notice. The report is divided into four parts: domestic and foreign academic costs and domestic and foreign medical costs.

It was decided to use these general categories for each library system, rather than to apply more specific subject categories, for three strategic reasons. The domestic and foreign books and serials categories represent all of the library system collections for all formats. Cost data would be available for the four categories on a consistent, timely and continuing basis. The categories preserved the maximum flexibility for each library and minimized the maintenance and analysis of data required each year for calculation of the index.

In order to implement a multi-part index a base year must be selected against which all changes are measured. The categories that are to be measured must be defined and the costs of the base year distributed against the total expenditures or costs of that year. Tables 1 defines the mechanism for building a price index.

Table 2 provides an example of a *Classic Index*, that is one that does not change the percentage distribution of costs from that of the base year. This is the usual form of an index as used by the Higher Education Price Index and the Consumer Price Index. In order to update an index the base year is changed after a period of time and costs are measured against the new base year.

The Adjusted Index shown in Table 3 is that used by Ohio State University to calculate the annual materials index figures. Although the original agreement was to maintain a Classic Index, it was clear that such an arrangement would require regular updating to maintain purchasing power. Financial Management established the principle of using an adjusted index that reflected *actual* expenditure

## TABLE 1

### Indexing Materials Budgets

### How to Build A Price Index

A price index is a mechanism for tracking price changes over time. It measures the changes against a constant array of items. To establish a price index, based on the Higher Education Price Index model and specific to your library, there are several basic steps. Once the model is established all that is required is to change the appropriate data each year.

1. Establish a base year against which all changes will be measured.

2. Define the categories of prices that you wish to measure.

3. Distribute base year expenditures across the categories identified.

4. Define the sources of price change data. These may be from internal library sources or from external published and recognized sources.

5. Multiply each category percentage by the percentage price change to be applied.

6. Add the resulting percentages across the categories to generate the annual over-all price change for library materials.

The above methodology is a *classic index*. To develop an *adjusted index* that more readily reflects immediate past fiscal year expenditures, make the following changes.

1. Define the categories of prices that you wish to measure.

2. Distribute expenditures across the categories identified. *This distribution will change each year as your expenditures change.*

3. Apply the price change data in steps 5-6 above.

## TABLE 2

### Example: **Classic Index**

|  | Serials | | Monographs | | Total |
| --- | --- | --- | --- | --- | --- |
|  | Domestic | Foreign | Domestic | Foreign |  |
| Base Year Distribution | 25% | 25% | 25% | 25% | 100% |
| Price change as reflected in source data | 10% | 25% | 5% | −10% |  |
| Percent change | .025% | .0625% | .0125% | −.025% | **+12.5%** |

Index price change according to classic distribution of expenditures and experienced price changes yields expenditure increase of **12.5%**. This change can be either positive or negative based on the price increase or decrease data applied to all categories.

distributions each year and calculated the final yearly index figure based on the most recent annual expenditures.

With the mechanism, data and process defined over a period of several months of negotiation, a procedure was established and the libraries understood that it had been approved. Unfortunately, that was not the case and library funding was once again a victim of administrative and budgetary pressures. At this point three of the major participants in the process changed. The University had a new president, a new provost and an acting vice president for finance. With these appointments in place and the plight of the libraries becoming more and more of a campus issue, agreement was reached and a formal document was signed in December 1990. Thirty-two months of education, frustration and creative negotiation finally resulted in an agreed upon mechanism for generating annual adjustments to the library materials budgets. It provides a mechanism, based on published index figures, that will maintain

## TABLE 3

### Example: Adjusted Index

|  | Serials | | Monographs | | Total |
|---|---|---|---|---|---|
|  | Domestic | Foreign | Domestic | Foreign |  |
| Adjusted Year Distribution | 30% | 40% | 25% | 5% | 100% |
| Price change as reflected in source data | 10% | 25% | 5% | −5% |  |
| Percent change | .03% | .10% | .01% | −.0025% | **+14.25%** |

Index price change according to adjusted distribution based on true expenditures yields a change of **+14.25%**.

purchasing power capacity. It reflects the currency concerns that are such an integral complication of research library funding. The Index does not provide for expansion or new program funds which must be sought through the University budget review process. The Index does, however, free the Libraries from the need to argue for the annual increases required to survive at present levels. Realistically, we must also realize that the index stipulated funding levels may be funded only if the University believes that it has the monies to do so.

Although the limits of budgetary support provided by the Index do not actually increase our funding levels within the university as a whole, the completion of and agreement with the process by the Libraries, Academic Affairs, and Financial Management greatly improves the chances of maintaining current levels of collection development. It is also significant in verifying the University's recognition of the importance of library resources and the economic vagaries to which they are subjected.

The day of the paperless (and libraryless) world is not yet here. Certainly technological changes are making an increasing impact on scholarly communication and in the educational process. Computer centers, the faculty, students and the library are becoming "increasingly intertwined."[16] But sole reliance on electronics and document delivery are still in the future and even when that day arrives information will still cost money. Someone must own it and be willing to provide it. Over time, libraries have proven to be the most reliable source for the continued provision, care, and preservation of the historical record. That is unlikely to change in the future. So, whether libraries are inside walls or only inside a fibre optic strand, information budgets, whatever their names, must still be maintained, strengthened, and defended in the organizational setting. An agreed upon methodology of cost justification and support is an efficient, effective, and appropriate means of generating institutional budgeting decisions over time.

## NOTES

1. *University Libraries and Scholarly Communication: A Study Prepared for the Andrew W. Mellon Foundation.* By Anthony Cummings et al. Washington, D.C.: Association of Research Libraries for The Andrew Mellon Foundation, Nov. 1992, p. 84. 205 p.

2. Adler, Prudence. "ARL Statistics Reflect Impact of Rising Prices," *ARL Newsletter*, March 1993, p. 6-7.

3. Bucknall, Carolyn. "Balancing collections, balancing budgets in academic libraries," *Journal of Library Administration*, 14(3),1991, p. 133.

4. Shaughnessy, Thomas W. "Management Strategies for Financial Crises," *Journal of Library Administration*, 10(1), 1989. p. 5.

5. Munn, Robert F. "The Bottomless Pit, or the Academic Library as Viewed from the Administration Building," *College and Research Libraries*, 50(6), November 1989, p. 637.

6. Munn, p. 637.

7. Berry, John N. "Acquisitions and collection development: A perspective from the top," *Acquisitions '90: Conference on Acquisitions, Budgets, and Collections.* St. Louis, Mo.: Genaway & Assocs., 1990, p. 4.

8. Moore, Susan and Donald E. Schauder. "Towards 2001: An examination of the present and future roles of libraries in relation to economic and social trends," *Journal of Library Administration*, 14(1), 1991, p. 19.

9. Houbeck, Robert L. "Listening to the Technology: Or, Libraries and the Higher Capitalism," *Journal of Library Administration*, 16(3), 1992, p. 74.

10. Garlock, Gayle. Personal communication, February 1993.

11. Clack, Mary E. and Sally Williams. "Using Locally and Nationally Produced Periodical Price Indexes in Budget Preparation," *College and Research Libraries*, 27(4), Oct./Dec. 1983, p. 345-356.

12. *Higher Education Price Indexes*. Washington, D.C.: Research Associates of Washington. (Title changed to *Inflation Measures for Schools & Colleges*, 1991- ).

13. ALCTS Library Materials Price Index Committee. "North American Academic Books: Average Prices and Price Indexes," *Bowker Annual Library and Book Trade Almanac*. New Providence, N.J.: Bowker.

14. Pletzke, Linda. "Library of Congress Average Foreign Book Prices," Private correspondence. (Occasionally published in the *Library of Congress Newsletter*).

15. Davidson, Robert. "Comparison of Foreign and Domestic Journal Price Data," Faxon Company.

16. *Preferred Futures for Libraries: A Summary of Six Workshops with University Provosts and Library Directors*. Stanford, CA: Research Libraries Group. 1992?, p. 16.

# Access vs. Ownership: What Is Most Cost Effective in the Sciences

Anthony W. Ferguson
Kathleen Kehoe

No library can own everything wanted by its patrons. Nevertheless, most research libraries have traditionally tried to own as much as possible and borrow as little as possible because owning an item provides faster patron access than waiting to borrow or purchase it upon demand. However, spiraling acquisitions costs have caused libraries to rethink how much information they can own and how much they will borrow or purchase from document delivery services.

At Columbia, we have not been able to compare how the costs of borrowing and document delivery compare with ownership. The purpose of this report is to compare these costs using data collected about monographs and periodicals not owned by Columbia. Admittedly, ownership versus access cost analysis is only one-half of the equation. Information about the speed of access to information is as

---

Anthony W. Ferguson is Associate University Librarian, Columbia University, New York, NY. Kathleen Kehoe is Reference/Collection Development Librarian, Science and Engineering Division, Columbia University.

The research reported in the paper is a component of a larger study of the information needs of scientists in Biology, Physics, and Electrical Engineering conducted at Columbia University between 1990 and 1992. Kathleen Kehoe collected the data for this paper and Anthony W. Ferguson wrote the paper.

[Haworth co-indexing entry note]: "Access vs. Ownership: What Is Most Cost Effective in the Sciences." Ferguson, Anthony W., and Kathleen Kehoe. Co-published simultaneously in *Journal of Library Administration* (The Haworth Press, Inc.) Vol. 19, No. 2, 1993, pp. 89-99: and: *Declining Acquisitions Budgets: Allocation, Collection Development and Impact Communication* (ed: Sul H. Lee) The Haworth Press, Inc., 1993, pp. 89-99. Multiple copies of this article/chapter may be purchased from The Haworth Document Delivery Center [1-800-3-HAWORTH; 9:00 a.m. - 5:00 p.m. (EST)].

© 1993 by The Haworth Press, Inc. All rights reserved.

important when deciding what should be owned or what should be accessed upon demand. Additional studies are underway to compare the speed of access using these alternate forms of access and patron attitudes about their relative acceptability.

## *FINDINGS*

### *Volume of Requests*

Information was collected on 1519 interlibrary loan and commercial document delivery requests processed between January 1991 and September 1992 for the faculty and graduate students from the Biology, Physics, and Electrical Engineering departments. Eighty-five percent of the requests were for periodicals, and 15 percent were for monographs. (See Table 1.)

Most of the requests were for unique titles. For 72% of the periodicals, only a single article was requested and over 92% of the monographs were requested only once. There were nonetheless 162 periodicals for which there were 2-3 articles requested and 49 periodicals for which there were four or more requests. Only in this last range of requests would the question of copyright infringement become an issue. Commercial document delivery services which pay copyright fees circumvents the problem while reliance upon traditional channels of interlibrary loan could be a problem. (See Table 2.)

### *Cost Comparisons: Access and Ownership*

An attempt was made to compare the fully loaded costs of ownership with the costs of accessing the requested materials through

Table 1

Volume of Periodicals and Monographs Requested

| Medium | Number | Percent of Total |
|---|---|---|
| Periodicals Articles | 1,284 | 85% |
| Monographs | 235 | 15% |
| Totals | 1,519 | 100% |

### Table 2

### Request Frequency:
### Periodicals and Monographs Compared

| No. Times Requested | No. Periodicals Titles | Percent of Total Periodicals Titles | No. Monograph Titles | Percent of Total Monograph Titles |
|---|---|---|---|---|
| 1 | 534 | 72% | 226 | 96.3% |
| 2 | 117 | 16% | 8 | 3.5% |
| 3 | 45 | 6% | 1 | 0.2% |
| 4 to 9 | 38 | 5% | 0 | 0% |
| 10< | 11 | 1% | 0 | 0 |
| Totals | 745 | 100% | 235 | 100% |

interlibrary loan or purchasing them from document delivery services. (See Appendix A for how the fully loaded interlibrary loan costs were calculated.) While there were a number of methodological problems associated with comparing costs, the following analysis approximates the relative differences between these two modes of meeting user needs. (See Appendix B for the methodological compromises made in order to complete this analysis.)

### *Monographs*

The costs associated with owning a monograph for its first use were clearly higher than for accessing it when needed. The purchase price, and the acquisitions processing and cataloging costs associated with the purchase of the 235 monographs borrowed, without regard to long term storage and preservation costs, would have cost the Libraries $33,370 in 1991 dollars instead of the $6,086 the Libraries spent borrowing them. Adding in storage and preservation costs would only add to the costs of ownership. (See Table 3.)

### *Periodicals*

While subscription price differences for the three disciplines influence the degree to which ownership costs exceed borrowing or document delivery charges, for most of the periodicals studied, it

Table 3

Fully Loaded Monograph Purchasing and Borrowing Costs Compared

| No. Times Requested | Number of Monographs | Estimated Purchase Costs (1) | Estimated Borrowing Costs (2) |
|---|---|---|---|
| 1 | 226 | $32,092 | $5,853 |
| 2 | 8 | $1,136 | $207 |
| 3 | 1 | $142 | $26 |
| 4 to 9 | 0 | $0 | $0 |
| 10< | 0 | $0 | $0 |
| Totals | 235 | $33,370 | $6,086 |

(1) Estimated purchase costs of $142 per volume based upon an average list price of $83 per volume and $59 per volume for acquisitions and cataloging costs.

(2) Estimated per volume borrowing cost of $25.90 based upon figures recently developed for the ARL/RLG ILL cost study.

was cheaper to access upon demand than to own in anticipation of need. Only when ten or more articles from a particular title were ordered did the costs of owning and acquiring on demand become nearly equal. The degree to which acquisition upon demand was less expensive than ownership also appeared to be a function of the degree to which the articles could be acquired more cheaply elsewhere in the Columbia system or through traditional channels of interlibrary loan than by resorting to a more expensive document delivery service. We estimated the fully loaded borrowing costs from other Columbia libraries or through interlibrary loan at $27 per article and $39 for each article acquired from a commercial document delivery service because the $39 figure includes both internal processing charges and the fees charged by the service.

*Biology:* The largest number of requests were processed for Biology Library users. Because subscription costs greatly exceeded access costs, the data indicates it was 21 times more expensive to subscribe than to acquire articles upon demand for the 423 periodicals for which only a single request was made. This difference might have been greater except that the subject overlap between the Biology Library and Columbia's Health Sciences Library meant that 965 of the 1062 requests were supplied at a lower cost than going through a commercial document delivery service. For biology, there were some periodicals titles (11), which would have been as cheap to own as to borrow or purchase from a document delivery service because of sufficient article demand. (See Table 4.)

*Physics:* The fewest number of transactions processed were for Physics Library patrons. Because there was little if any useful subject overlap between the Physics Library and any other Columbia library and because traditional interlibrary loan was judged to be too slow, all of the 48 articles involved more expensive document delivery service charges. Coupled with a $1,202 average subscription price, it was 31 times more expensive to subscribe than to acquire articles upon demand for the 20 periodicals for which only a single request was made. (See Table 5.)

*Electrical Engineering:* The transactions processed by the Engineering Library for electrical engineering material patrons fell in number between those ordered for Biology and Physics libraries researchers. While not all of these were acquired from commercial services, 146 of the total were ordered in this way. With an average subscription cost of $728 per periodicals title, the data suggests it was 20 times more expensive to subscribe than to acquire articles

Table 4

Biology: Subscription and Access Costs Compared

| No. Times Requested | Number of Periodicals Titles | Total Articles Requested | Estimated Subscription Costs* | Estimatd Access Costs** | Difference Between Costs | Subscription to Access Ratio |
|---|---|---|---|---|---|---|
| 1 | 423 | 423 | $244,917 | $11,421 | $233,496 | 21 |
| 2 | 94 | 188 | $54,426 | $5,076 | $49,350 | 11 |
| 3 | 35 | 105 | $20,265 | $2,835 | $17,430 | 7 |
| 4 to 9 | 31 | 190 | $17,949 | $5,130 | $12,819 | 3 |
| 10< | 11 | 156 | $6,369 | $4,212 | $2,157 | 2 |
| Totals | 594 | 1062 | $343,926 | $28,674 | $315,252 | 12 |

*An average of $579 per title, based upon an average 1991 per title subscription price of $520 and a $59 per volume acquisitions processing cost.

**An average of $27 per article acquired, based upon fully loaded cost estimates of $26 for each article acquired from another Columbia System library or through traditional interlibrary loan channels and $39 for each article acquired from a commercial document delivery service (x articles).

## Table 5

### Physics: Subscription and Access Costs Compared

| No. Times Requested | Number of Periodicals Titles | Total Articles Requested | Estimated Subscription Costs* | Estimated Access Costs** | Difference Between Costs | Subscription to Access Ratio |
|---|---|---|---|---|---|---|
| 1 | 20 | 20 | $24,020 | $780 | $23,240 | 31 |
| 2 | 2 | 4 | $2,402 | $156 | $2,246 | 15 |
| 3 | 3 | 9 | $3,603 | $351 | $3,252 | 10 |
| 4 to 9 | 3 | 15 | $3,603 | $585 | $3,018 | 6 |
| 10< | 0 | 0 | $0 | $0 | $0 | |
| Totals | 28 | 48 | $33,628 | $1,872 | $31,756 | 18 |

*An average of $1201 per title, based upon 1991 subscription prices for all 28 periodicals and a $59 per volume acquisitions processing cost.

**Since all 48 articles were acquired from commercial document delivery services, the average cost was the estimated fully loaded cost of $39 for each article.

upon demand for the 91 periodicals for which only a single request was made. (See Table 6.)

## Subset Analysis

The findings above assert that it is cheaper to access these periodicals at Columbia than to own them. In 1987, because of budget limitations, Columbia cut a number of periodicals subscriptions. Journals of lesser importance were cancelled while more important journals were kept because it was believed that access costs would be less than subscription costs. Using the data we collected for the Scientific Information Project, we were able to test this assumption by analyzing 10 titles that had been cancelled in 1987. Indeed, subscription costs were higher than access charges for eight of these titles. Subscription costs to access ratios, however, were significantly smaller than for the Biology, Physics, and Electrical Engineering journals just discussed. This may be due to the fact that these ten journals had been once judged important enough to be in the collection and were, therefore, comparatively more important to Columbia's uses than the larger group of journals, most of which were never in the collection. When we examine each title the significance

Table 6

Electrical Engineering:
Subscription and Access Costs Compared

| No. Times Requested | Number of Periodicals Titles | Total Articles Requested | Estimated Subscription Costs* | Estimated Access Costs** | Difference Between Costs | Subscription to Access Ratio |
|---|---|---|---|---|---|---|
| 1 | 91 | 91 | $66,248 | $3,276 | $62,972 | 20 |
| 2 | 21 | 42 | $15,288 | $1,512 | $13,776 | 10 |
| 3 | 7 | 21 | $5,096 | $756 | $4,340 | 7 |
| 4 to 9 | 4 | 20 | $2,912 | $720 | $2,192 | 4 |
| 10 < | 0 | 0 | $0 | $0 | $0 | |
| Totals | 123 | 174 | $89,544 | $6,264 | $83,280 | 14 |

*An average of $728 per title, based upon an average 1991 per title subscription price of $669 and an average $59 per volume acquisitions processing cost.

**An average of $27 per article acquired, based upon fully loaded cost estimates of $26 for each article acquired from another Columbia system library or through traditional interlibrary loan channels and $39 for each article acquired from a commercial document delivery service.

of cost and use factors becomes clearer. In some specific cases it would be cheaper to own than to access. For example, *The American Journal of Physiology, Part C*, cost only $209 per year and had 10 articles requested during the test period. This was also true for *Biochemistry and Cell Biology* which cost $270 annually and experienced 6 requests. In both of these cases the subscription price to access cost ratio was balanced or even in favor of subscribing. For *Physica Status Solidi, Part A*, on the other hand, an annual subscription price of 1,183 and only four requests produced an 8 to 1 subscription price to access cost ratio.( See Table 7.)

## *In and Out of Scope*

All of the monographs and periodicals titles requested were also analyzed by the subject specialist librarians to determine whether or not they fell within the collecting scope of the library. Eighty percent of the periodicals titles requested were in scope while 40 percent of the monographs were seen as appropriate for the collection. (See Table 8.) Interestingly, the out of scope periodicals were sig-

## TABLE 7

Ownership and Access Cost Compared:
Journals Cancelled in 1987

| Title | Number of Articles Requested | Estimated Subscription Costs* | Estimated Access Costs** | Difference Between Costs | Subscription to Access Ratio |
|---|---|---|---|---|---|
| Physica Status Solidi, Part A | 4 | $1,183 | $156 | $1,027 | 8 |
| Oecologia | 9 | $2,190 | $351 | $1,839 | 6 |
| Radiophysics & Quantum Electronics | 7 | $974 | $273 | $701 | 4 |
| Physica Scripta | 8 | $1,044 | $312 | $732 | 3 |
| Journal of Applied Bacteriology | 5 | $496 | $195 | $301 | 3 |
| Archiv Fur Protistenkunde | 3 | $296 | $117 | $179 | 3 |
| Canadian Journal of Physiology | 5 | $346 | $195 | $151 | 2 |
| Applied & Environmental Microbiology | 5 | $309 | $195 | $114 | 2 |
| Biochemistry and Cell Biology | 6 | $270 | $234 | $36 | 1 |
| Am. Journal Physiology, Part C. | 10 | $209 | $390 | ($181) | −1 |
| Totals | 62 | $7,317 | $2,418 | $4,899 | 3 |

*Based upon actual 1991 subscription prices and a $59 per volume acquisitions processing cost. **For the sake of this analysis, the $39 document delivery charge was used.

Table 8

The Scope of Materials Requested

| Scope | No. Monographs | Percent of Total Monographs | No. Periodicals Articles | Percent of Total Periodicals |
|---|---|---|---|---|
| In Scope | 80 | 34.04% | 1167 | 80.48% |
| Out of Scope | 155 | 65.96% | 283 | 19.52% |
| Totals | 235 | 100% | 1450 | 100% |

nificantly cheaper than the in-scope titles. The average in-scope periodical was $440 while the out-of-scope title was $304. This same direction is apparent when comparing the cost of the in-scope but not owned periodicals with those owned. Our average owned periodical averaged $610. It seems that the more important the journal is to Columbia's users, the higher will be its subscription price. Some have suggested that journals are priced more in terms of their importance to the field than because of production costs. This deserves further investigation.

## *CONCLUSIONS*

Materials borrowed or purchased on demand to meet user needs appear to mirror the circulation patterns of materials owned by the Science libraries: periodicals are used more than monographs. If cost is the only consideration, this data suggests, it is significantly less expensive to purchase periodicals articles from document delivery services or borrow them through interlibrary loan than to buy them in anticipation of need. The extent to which this is true, however, depends upon the price and use characteristics of each title. Stated as a rule of thumb, it is better to access than to own if the cost of borrowing (in 1991 a maximum of $39 per unit for commercial document delivery) is less than the cost of subscribing. Consequently, one must look at each periodical title individually to make this decision. Monographs not owned by Columbia were also found to be cheaper to access than to own.

Cost, however, is not the only factor to be considered when building library collections. Our studies of unbound periodicals use show that browsing of new periodicals issues is a very important research activity. While it might be cheaper to buy only what researchers identify as needed from footnotes or from indexes and abstracting services, total reliance upon this tactic would deprive our users of the opportunity to find information in the way they have found to be most successful: browsing. We determined, therefore, to experiment with electronic bibliographic access to the contents of periodicals to find out if it could serve as an effective substitute. We also decided to experiment with document delivery services to discover if their speed and quality of image are acceptable to our users. These experiments have been designed and are being conducted during 1993 with support from the University.

If electronic browsing and document delivery could substitute or indeed be viewed as superior to the browsing and photocopying activities that are currently employed by most science library users, the whole research library paradigm that has dominated for the past 100 years will be changed. Instead of buying in anticipation of need, libraries will spend more of their funds on access and delivery. If not, libraries will need to reexamine their current momentum toward electronic access instead of library ownership in print or electronic mediums.

## APPENDIXES

### Appendix A

Columbia University Fully Loaded Borrowing Costs Per Document

| | |
|---|---|
| Supervisory | $4.01 |
| Non Supervisory Staff | $18.46 |
| Network Fees | $1.65 |
| Delivery | $1.27 |
| Supplies | $0.07 |
| Equipment and Software | $0.19 |
| Rental and Maintenance | $0.02 |
| Purchasing Fees Charged | $0.23 |
| Total | $25.90 |

(Source: ARL/RLG Cost Study–Preliminary Report, October 15, 1992)

## Appendix B

### Methodological Compromises

Several methodological problems were encountered which required conceptual compromises. First of all, when you truly attempt to compare the cost of purchasing a 1941 biology monograph with borrowing it in 1991 you are confronted with a number of problems. Should you assume you could buy the out-of-print 1941 imprint for the same cost as a 1991 biology monograph or should you add to the 1941 actual price the estimated cost of what would have cost your library to house it for 50 intervening years. Knowing that this was to be a conceptual exercise we opted for the former and rejected the latter. We also decided to ignore thoughts about what it would cost to continue to own the monograph for another 50 years or in addition what preservation costs might be incurred. We did, however, add to the average monograph purchase costs what we estimated to be the processing costs for each title. This compromise allowed us to compare estimated 1991 purchase costs with 1991 borrowing costs.

The second major methodological problem involved periodicals. While it is comparatively easy to compute in 1991 the fully loaded costs of borrowing or purchasing from a document delivery company a 1942 article from a journal, it is very difficult to establish what should be the 1991 ownership costs. Should it be the cost of subscribing to a single current year of the periodical? Should the cost of the entire run of the periodical be used since predicting which backrun volume of a periodical will be needed is impossible? Once again, in order to get a conceptual handle on the relative differences between the ownership and access costs, we compromised and compared the sum of 1991 subscription and processing costs with the sum of interlibrary loan or document delivery costs.

A third problem related to the simple fact that we had 18 months of request data but were using only 12 month subscription costs for the periodicals subscription data. We could have dropped 6 months of the data to compare two 12-month clusters of data, but our numbers were already low for Physics and we did not want to further weaken what we knew about what titles were actually needed by our patrons. Alternatively, we could have added another six months of subscription costs, but with changes in the value of the dollar, we were wary about introducing yet another variable. In the end, we felt that the request figures were only a picture of what was requested in one arbitrary period of time. We knew from our bound periodicals studies that the amount a title was used in one quarter was not exactly predictive of how much it might be used in a future quarter. We viewed, therefore, the request data as relative but nonetheless grounded in reality.

# Toward a Calculus
# of Collection Development

## Charles Hamaker

Kendon Stubbs retells the story of the Parisian bistro that served a delicious but amazingly inexpensive rabbit stew. Someone asked the proprietor how he could afford to sell his rabbit stew so cheaply. "Well," he said, "I do put a little horsemeat too. But I mix them 50-50: one rabbit, one horse" (Kendon Stubbs. To ARL Directors, 6 September, 1992).

In trying to understand the problems facing the scholarly communication system right now, its hard to tell at times what we are seeing, the rabbit or the horse in the mix of fact and fiction that is circulating.

Defining the problem has become a way of life in the war of words. For Karen Hunter, a vice president of Elsevier, the largest STM (Scientific, Technical and Medical) publisher in the world, the problem looked like too many rabbits.

In a letter in September of 1987 responding to concerns about Elsevier's pricing strategies covered in a meeting at Yale University, Hunter said:

> In many respects the universities—in continuing to reward rapid, frequent publication—are creating their libraries problems

---

Charles Hamaker is Assistant Dean, Collection Development, Louisiana State University Libraries, Baton Rouge, LA.

[Haworth co-indexing entry note]: "Toward a Calculus of Collection Development." Hamaker, Charles. Co-published simultaneously in *Journal of Library Administration* (The Haworth Press, Inc.) Vol. 19, No. 2, 1993, pp. 101-123; and: *Declining Acquisitions Budgets: Allocation, Collection Development and Impact Communication* (ed: Sul H. Lee) The Haworth Press, Inc., 1993, pp. 101-123. Multiple copies of this article/chapter may be purchased from The Haworth Document Delivery Center [1-800-3-HAWORTH; 9:00 a.m. - 5:00 p.m. (EST)].

themselves. This means we all–university administrators, authors, publishers and librarians will have to be involved in seeking long-term solutions.

Yet, in 1991 in a move that suggested the problem was the horses were the major ingredient in the stew of scholarly communication, Elsevier purchased the third largest STM publisher in the world, Robert Maxwell's Pergamon Press. The sale price was reported as $765 Million ($440 Million pounds) in cash. What was astounding was that Elsevier paid for this purchase out of cash reserves. They didn't have to go to the banks for the largest STM publisher merger in history! And, even though in 1987 Elsevier tried to suggest that STM publishing was only "part" of their profit mix, in fact in the last 2 years the company has bragged in its annual reports that specifically the portion of their business aimed at the Academic market was the most profitable, so profitable in fact that for the last 20 years their annual return on capital employed has been about 20%. In 1986 net income after taxes as a percentage of sales was about 8% and last year that figure was closer to 12%.

The primary answer to the question of why journal prices have escalated well above any traditional measure of price increase (CPI for example) has been that there has been an explosive growth in article production, article proliferation.

This first graph shows the cumulative effect of CPI from 1982 to 1989 and a standard "periodical price index" which is an extremely conservative tool for measuring price increases in periodical publications (see Figure 1). Actual experience with serial price increases in research libraries has been a bit different from this broad based index (more on that later) (see Figure 2).

And there are lots of analysts who imply we should expect price increases for access to scientific literature to be well above CPI or GNP figures. For example, John Naisbitt in *Megatrends* suggested that Scientific and Technical information increases by about 13% a year, doubling in 5.5 years. Other statements from other sources suggest a doubling period of 12 years, or 8 years. Naisbitt says when computer produced information is included the doubling period currently is at 20 months. The grandaddy so to speak of this school of thought is Derek De Sola Price. In *Big Science Little*

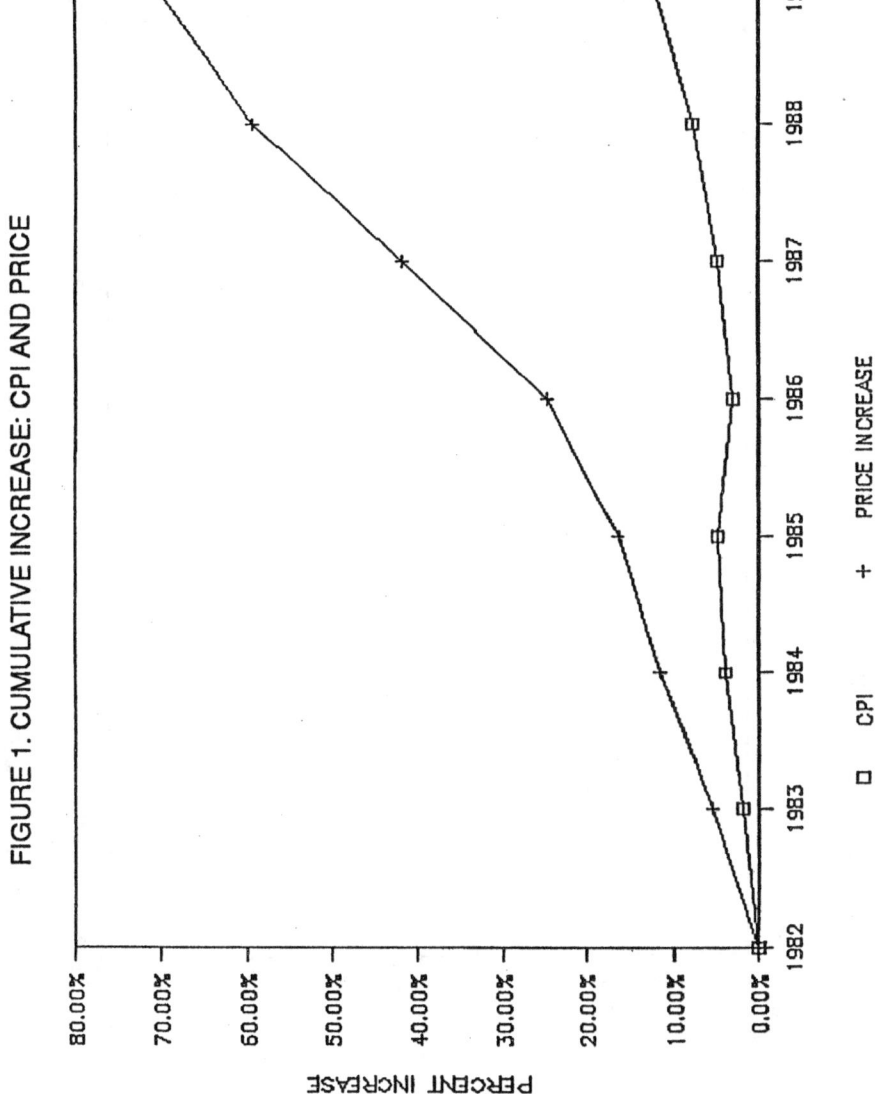

FIGURE 1. CUMULATIVE INCREASE: CPI AND PRICE

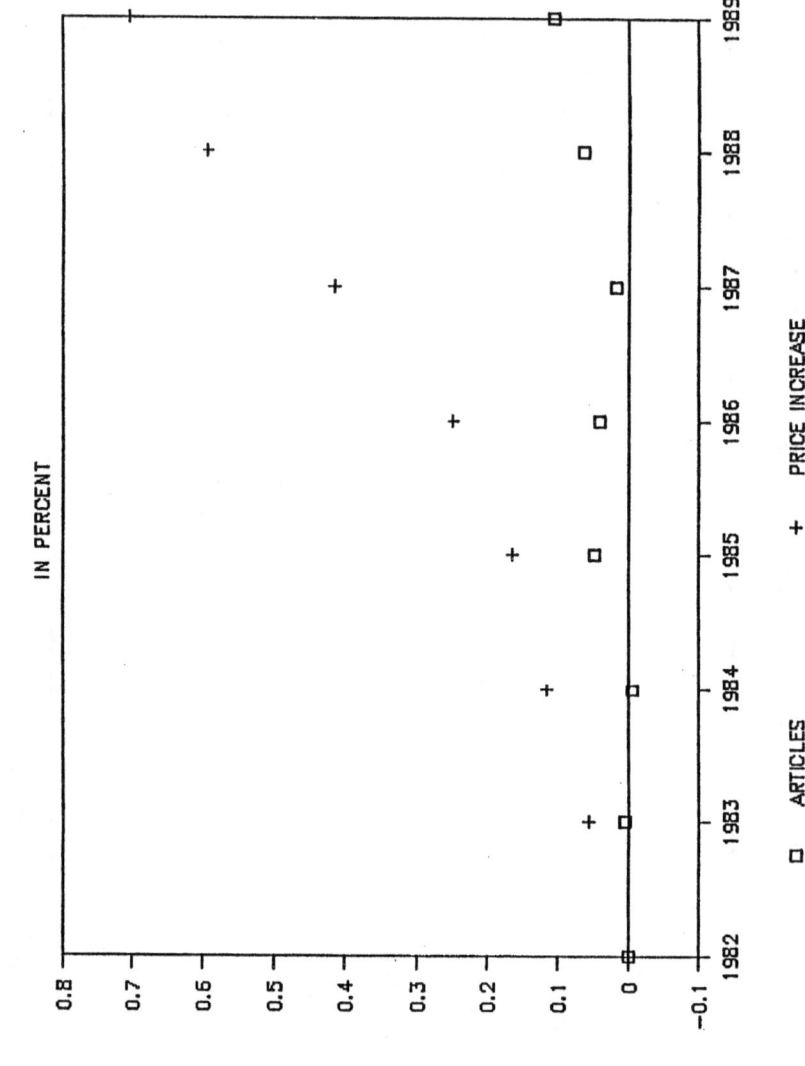
FIGURE 2. ARTICLE PRODUCTION VS. PRICE INCREASE

*Science*, he argued that scientific and technical information has doubled every 15 years for over three centuries, an annual growth rate of about 5 percent.

With numbers this disparate, what growth in the scientific literature actually is and how much it "should" cost to maintain access to that literature looks like a wide open question.

Another perspective is suggested in the growth rate in scholarly or academic book titles. New books available in the U.S. market in 1982 totalled about 23,000 and had an average price of $23.05. In 1991-92 the average price was $46.29 and new title availability was around 34,000. Thus the number of books increased about 44% in the decade and the average price increased about 65%. To maintain a constant "percentage of literature coverage" in monographs, expenditures in the decade would have had to double. In fact, for ARL libraries, number of books purchased in just the last 5 years have decreased about 15%. One of the major casualties of what have been called the "Serial" wars has been access to books in North America's academic and research libraries.

In fact, the increased price of journals and other serials in ARL libraries has been much higher than any published index suggests. ARL has tracked amounts spent on periodicals in ARL member libraries since 1975. And, as Ann Okerson reported at the Oklahoma Conference in 1991, "the subscription price of serials has been increasing on average, by 10% per year compounded since 1975." She notes: "the 10% is shocking because over 16 years the price of serials subscriptions in academic libraries increased by over fourfold." (Ann Okerson "The Older Order Changes; A Plan for Action" *Journal of Library Administration* 16,3 (1992):4-5.) The accelerating cost of scholarly information matches two other exponentially growing components of our society thought to be out of control: medical care costs and doing "big science" projects.

LSU's experience parallels the experience of other research libraries. In 1979 total serial expenditures were reported for Middleton of $552,000. In 1991-92 or expenditures for a stable list of titles (although there is some indication the number of paid subscriptions has declined radically since 1982) was $1.9 million.

Another way of asking this question about serials expenditures is to use an implicit deflator to see what the actual increase in cost for serials was in "constant dollars." In 1982 constant dollars, serials expenditures have grown by 113% (while R&D expenditures have grown by 108%) (Kendon Stubbs, 1992). ARL libraries, have continued to find whatever money it takes to maintain more or less the same number of serials each year, even though increase in the expenditures for serials have been "double" the increases in ordinary inflation since 1976) (Stubbs, 1992).

> Since the mid-1970's, in real terms, serials funding in ARL libraries has kept up with the expanding investment in research and development.

> The money ARL libraries has been spending on articles resulting from R&D has risen almost exactly as much as increase in the original R&D expenditures.

When we are talking about growth in R&D expenditures, the largest growth has not been in basic research, but in applied and developmental areas. In fact, Universities and Colleges perform the bulk of research in basic areas, while industry and the federal government itself preform the lion's share of research in applied and developmental fields. In 1982 constant dollars overall funding (from all sources) for all forms of R&D has increased about 38% from roughly $80 billion to $110 billion. In current dollars, that is from $80 billion to $145 billion, or roughly an *81%* increase from 82 to 1990. Remember that number! Once again, this tracks, the "index" increase in serial prices.

SO WHERE'S THE BEEF. Or is there really horsemeat in this stew? From this description it all looks like perfectly normal rabbits wouldn't you say?

In this context the answer that publishers have given libraries, and in some instances are still providing, is that this is a library problem–as recently as Nov. 7, 1992 two publishing consultants told an assembled group of librarians and publishers at a national conference the solution to the problem is for Libraries to go get more money. Publishers, they argued, are behaving in truly responsible fashion to handle the ever increasing tide of articles that is threatening to inundate them and their system.

But there is another side to this story. Kendon Stubbs suggests the fly in the ointment in his September letter to ARL directors.

> ... in its *Science and Engineering Indicators, 1991* the National Science Board Displays a table showing that from 1981 to 1987 the number of U.S. scientific and technical articles increase by only 2% while R&D expenditures in real dollars increased by 40%.

That statement has intrigued me every since I saw it. *Science and Engineering Indicators* provides some intriguing numbers. In tracking worldwide scientific article production, they depend on the ISI database for *Science Citation Index*. With a base of about 3,200 journals, SCI article counts from 1982 to 1987 grew by about 2%. From 1982 to 1989, the last date there is ISI data for, those 3,200 journals have a cumulative effect of increasing article production by about 11%. So with a stable "stable" of journals, or relatively so, though ISI does add new stars, and is generally thought of as providing the core indexing for science, there is no evidence of 5 year doubling periods, no evidence of 15 year doubling periods, in fact the overall growth over a 10 year period looks remarkably low, approaching Consumer Price Index numbers.

At LSU we decided to look at the data we had on hand to find out what happened in the journals we buy that are included in the mix the National Science Board used. They used data from ISI's databases and the 3,200 journals indexed there. We looked at 480 journals we received at LSU that have source items (i.e., number of "articles" or citable sources) noted in the *Journal Citation Reports* and for which we had 1983 and 1988 prices. We started with a larger universe of titles for which we had 1988 data but decided to use only titles where we had consistent pricing and source item data. Of the 480 titles, 156, a third, actually decreased in terms of source item counts and the decrease was significant, over 18%. The cost of those same journals to our library increased over the six year period by 63%. The annual rate of increase in price was therefore 8.46% and the annual rate of decrease in source items was −3.27%. For the other 324 titles, there was an increase in source item production of an annual rate of 4.77% (very close to that 5% the De Solla Price used) and an average annual rate of increase in price of 11.32%. Overall, however, for this group of titles–all 480– the source item count increased an average of 2.77% per year. Well below that magic 5% figure. And price increased an average 10.6% a year. Overall, the price of these 480 serials with their growth rate of under 3% increased 90% in the six years covered in the study while article growth was close to the growth in the Consumer Price Index. This data, if confirmed by a more systematic review of the ISI titles, has serious implications for this system we are all struggling with. Even when they have losers, publishers price their "losing" titles not much differently than their "winners." The real losers in this undifferentiated price war are researchers and libraries. From 1983 to 1988 the "difference" in the "growth" titles and the "losers" in terms of price was about 17%. Library budgets clearly are being raided whether there is an increase in production or not. With this doubling rate in *price* of about 6 years, libraries are being destroyed as cultural repositories of the literate word.

The parameters of the serials debate were radically challenged in 1986 and 1987 when we discovered that a very small number of titles and publishers represented disproportionate sums of our serials dollars. In November of 1986 LSU reported that about 20% of our subscriptions accounted for 72% of our expenditures. Several university libraries duplicated our study and found that about 10% of their titles accounted for 50% of expenditures in a range of academic libraries from the relatively small University of Missouri at St. Louis to the larger Universities of Hawaii and Michigan, and medium range institutions of Kent State and Clemson.

In the context of price increases, LSU learned that three publishers alone, accounting for about 488 serials out of the 11,000 subscriptions, were responsible for 43% of our price increase in 1986-87. So not only were there just a few titles affecting the overall mix of expenditures, there were even fewer titles with a major impact on price increase rates.

As an aside here, partially because of this and other research on questions of STM publishing, LSU has come under attack, an attack reported as "fact" in a recent issue of the Chronicle of Higher Education. A report published in the fall 1992 issue of *Publishing*

*Research Quarterly* noted that LSU library funding had not increased when research centers opened on the LSU campus. Dean Cargill has had a letter published in the *Chronicle* responding to that attack. The major attack however has been on ARL and its libraries generally. Essentially the argument is that overall library funding has not kept pace with R&D funding, therefore libraries, if they were funded properly would "properly" maintain serials collections for researchers. This is another version of go get more money.

Pergamon, Springer Verlag and Elsevier behavior have been a particular concern of mine over the last 6 years, and I have tracked not only prices but output per issue and per volume of their titles.

Here is a picture of Pergamon pricing and production for a significant portion of the Pergamon journals at LSU (see Figure 3). From 1982 to 1992 prices for these journals increased about 320% while number of volumes produced increased less than 10% (actually from 144 volumes to 154 volumes).

Well, that isn't a "good enough" observation. Say the publishers–well we increased numbers of issues, increased pages in volumes, this doesn't tell the whole story.

The second largest science publisher in the world is Springer Verlag. Although we don't have complete data, here is a look at 58 of the 101 journals we subscribe to at LSU (see Figure 4). As you can see, issue production doesn't much equate with price increase either. And in this instance because the major answer to those complaining librarians has been that most of your problem is currency fluctuation, I've shown percentage price increases in DM (German Marks) along with issue production. Price in dollars went from $25,000 in 1980 to $68,000 in 1991 (in 1987 they cost $39,000).

The third publisher of this triumvirate, Elsevier, actually does show some increases in production. In 1980, 105 titles (of the 205 we subscribe to) produced 449 volumes, and 1,482 issues at a price of $35,680. In 1992 those titles produced (will produce) 830 volumes and 2,823 issues with a total price of $140,000. For all Elsevier titles, in fact, the price in 1987 was about $120,000 and after canceling about 6% of the titles, our cost for 1993 would be over $260,000.

What is going on here, what is happening? Now this is certainly a

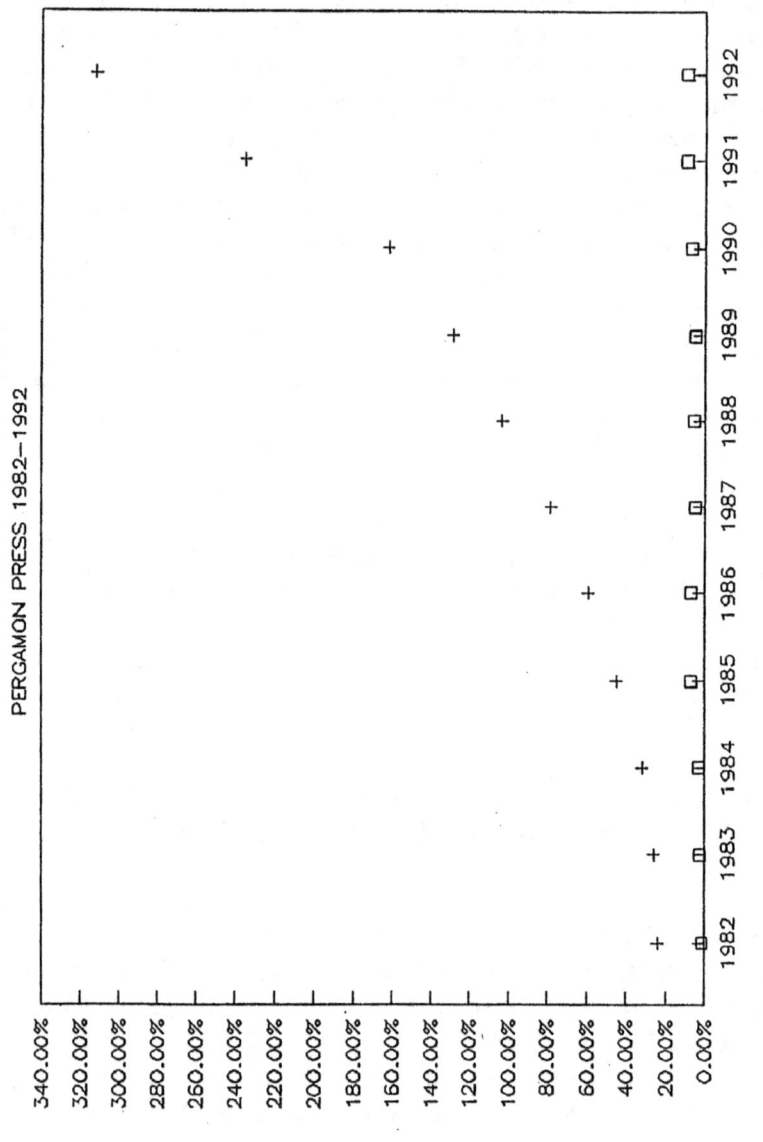

FIGURE 3. CUMULATIVE INCREASES COST AND VOLUMES
PERGAMON PRESS 1982–1992

FIGURE 4. SPRINGER VERLAG PERCENT INCREASE
ISSUES AND DM YEAR TO YEAR

Percent inc. issues
Percent inc. DM

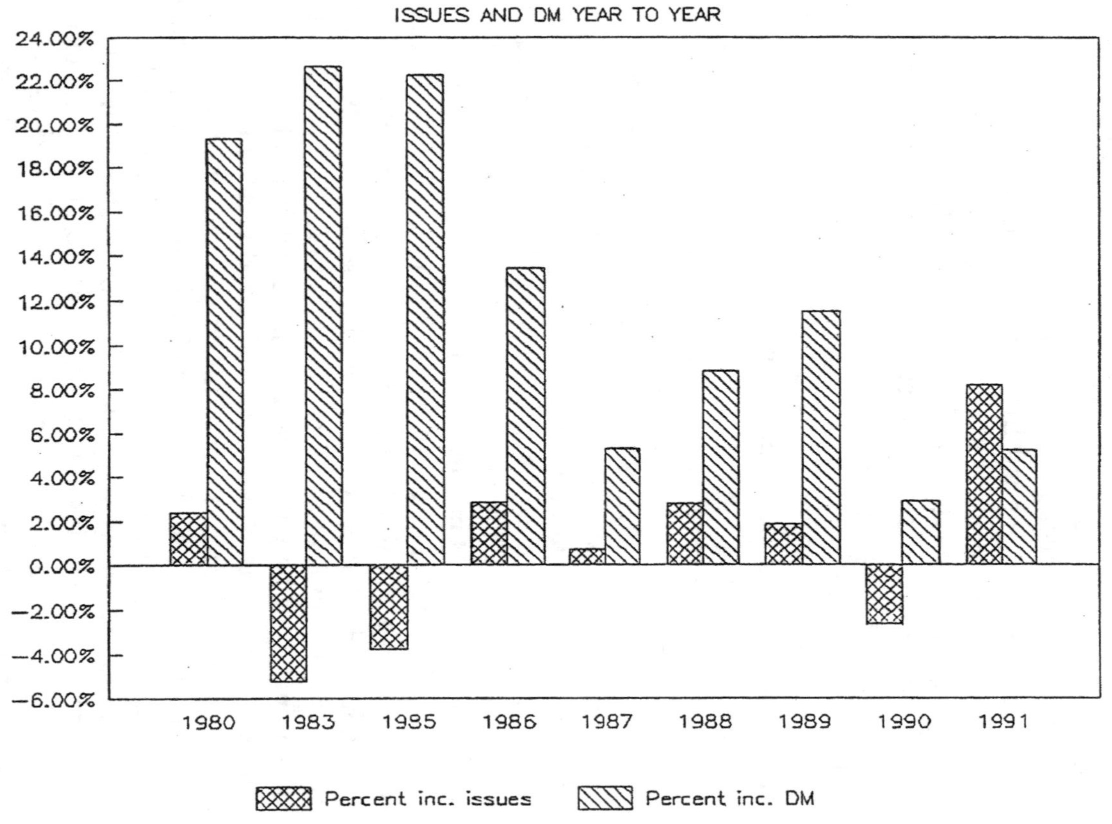

speculative area. There are all sorts of concerns such as how the ISI universe reflects reality and what shifts are taking place. We know by special index counts for example that the growth rates in some disciplines certainly are dynamic. Physics comes to mind immediately, and the Chemical literature. But as an hypothesis, given the Pergamon and Springer and Elsevier numbers, perhaps in a microcosm what we are seeing is not an explosion in articles, but a major shift going on as to where articles are published. That is, a major shift from society and association publications in some fields, towards the commercial presses.

And though this is a tenuous argument until we have more data, I would suggest that change is what we are about right now. Perhaps, the problem is explosion of "rabbits," i.e., article proliferation. Certainly some titles are facing it, and perhaps, as I am suggesting here, the problem is we have some very large horses affecting the stew.

Whatever the problem, the basic fact is that libraries have taken much of the burden of financing one of the underpinnings of scientific advance, journal publication. Even societies and associations have increasingly relied on subscriptions for funding things other than publications. With commercial presses showing how to make good money on STM publications, libraries have been pushed into a support role that they had not previously played. And the academy has been unable, ultimately to fund what is often referred to as a bottomless pit. Increasingly even librarians are stating that the answer to the problems we face is not more funds, but a fundamental rethinking of how the scientific literature is produced and purchased and used. In November, 1992, Fred Lynden of Brown University indicated Brown would no longer ask for library materials funding in excess of CPI or normal inflation levels. This signals an awareness and a commitment to contain explosive expenditures.

Over the last twenty years there has been a shift of responsibility for selection and paying for library purchases. Gone, in most institutions, are the days of departmental library allocations controlled by a "library representative." Most libraries have librarians with either full or part time responsibilities to provide selection and purchase decisions for library materials. This process ultimately divided the primary users of library materials from information regarding the price of library materials. It is sort of like needing a car when someone else is going to pay for it. You want the best car money can buy, especially since it isn't "your" money buying it. In the case of STM journals however, increasingly because of market share shifts over the last 20 years, the only cars generally available (and even they are made in limited numbers) are the Rolls Royces. And the budget to buy them with the kinds of pressures we have been describing, might be able to afford a good dependable family sedan. The problem is the sedans don't much exist anymore and when they do exist they don't have the amenities you need.

Economists describe this situation, and publishers have not been slow to grasp its significance, as Inelastic Demand. That is, for luxury items generally, high prices do not result in a lowering of demand for the item. So publishers have learned that 20, and 30 and 40 percent price increases do not generally effect the demand for their products. Libraries, as institutional customers, have continued to buy. Individual purchasers, for titles that are still aimed at the individual market, decline rapidly as price increases. Libraries have been price-insensitive, the individual market price-sensitive. This has lead to all sorts of marketing devices. If your library doesn't have a subscription you can't have one at the "individual" rate (a genteel form of blackmail?). Differential pricing, one rate for individuals another to libraries, with enormous differentials reported in the literature. Differential pricing between countries (a higher rate for U.S. libraries than for British Libraries (or vice-versa)). Country of origin versus country of sale pricing. And most recently from Springer Verlag, American libraries must purchase journals published in Germany through the U.S. office, no matter what vendor they use worldwide. A German vendor must buy German journals for American libraries through New York. These practices exacerbate already tense relationships between libraries and publishers.

How are libraries responding to this situation, and what directions is access to scholarly publishing likely to take in both the short and long term?

I have been describing what is clearly a systemic crisis. The major symptom is price escalation. Increasing journal cancellations and radical drops in book purchases are also symptoms. And not only the long run, but in the short term we are facing a system that is convulsing. Commercial publishers report their most expensive and most profitable titles are receiving the heaviest cancellation load. Monograph publishers are reporting print runs that a few years ago would have qualified the titles as rare books. And use of materials in libraries, if LSU is any example, is accelerating as demands on research, grantsmanship and on the quality of undergraduate education increase. There have been several calls for change, often though only librarians are hearing those calls. And this is a major problem. Libraries are consumers of scholarly information only in the fact that they are purchasing on behalf of others, and of society. Libraries are intermediaries. Faculty, researchers and students are the consumers (if in fact information can ever be said to be "consumed").

The first call for change, has been to inform major users of library materials about the systemic crisis facing scholarly information system. In particular, the pressures on the Serials Information Chain, a phrase coined in 1984 by the founders of NASIG (The North American Serials Information Group).

Secondly, details of the system are coming under increasing scrutiny from again, a systemic level. I call your attention to two different documents. The first, the Aqueduct agenda, from a group of librarians who met in Chapel Hill, NC, the second a draft of a model "University Policy Regarding Faculty Publication in Scholarly Journals" which was published in the *Newsletter on Serials Pricing Issues*.

For the rest of this presentation, I want to examine some of the implications of these two documents, and reactions to them.

First, however, I should note that in reaction to the "proliferation" argument some institutions are limiting the number of articles they will examine for tenure and promotion, or for funding grants. While primarily in Medical fields, this is an acknowledgement that quality not quantity should be the basic criteria for academic advancement and funding research. The Harvard Medical School is limiting articles it will look at for promotion and tenure decisions to 5. I understand that NIH is making similar restrictions.

What are the barriers to dissemination of scholarly information? The publisher answer has been money.

And in recognition of that, the Aqueduct document places

squarely in the public eye, the demand for journals, price and price history to be significant criteria for selection and cancellation decisions. This principle runs counter to much of the practice of the last twenty years. The "traditional" bibliographer, and to an extent the traditional faculty approach with journals, has been I make the decision about the quality and utility of the journal–the library figures out how to maintain payment. Even journal editors and publishers should be notified of the reasons for canceling journal titles. This practice which is clearly affecting some publishers, has resulted in an increased clamor, particularly from Elsevier and Pergamon who have sent letters to editors and in some instances editorial board members, claiming that the problem is libraries need more money. They have argued that total library budgets have not kept pace with R&D outlays. True enough, but as I have shown, Serials Expenditures certainly have kept pace with R&D outlays.

Items 7 and 9 on the Aqueduct agenda could easily be the most controversial points on the list.

> Share cancellation lists and criteria for cancellation within a consortium or region in order to promote cooperative collection development.

The theory of shared collection development has been around a long time. There is a prior example that worked. Targeting national cancellations of expensive European journals in 1933, the American Library Association and the Medical Library Association called on libraries to jointly cancel excessively expensive journals unless they decreased in price. To insure that at least one copy of each journal recommended for cancellation be available for use, the U.S. was divided into nine regions or zones, with one library in each zone assuming the responsibility to retain a given subscription. Charles Harvey Brown commenting on this scheme, expected it to grow. "It is to be hoped that the organization now being effected can later be used to consider the resources of American libraries and to obtain the acceptance by individual libraries of certain fields of certain classes of publications which they will collect exhaustively and make available to scholars generally. American librarians have been criticized for their failure to obtain such an understanding" (see Hamaker and Astle's chapter in volume 2 of *Advances in Serials Librarianship* for more background to this movement).

So the theory has been around. Why not the practice. Some attempt was made to "systematize collecting" through Conspectus development. That is generally recognized as the failure of the 80's. However, the AAP in a document from July of 1992 indicates that cooperative decisions, however reached, on serials titles would be illegal (see AAP Memorandum, July 28, 1992 issued by Barbara Meredith, Director PSP). In the House-Senate conference report for the 1976 copyright law revisions, some discussion is applicable to the problem of "subscription sharing" or as more commonly called, "resource sharing." The Senate in discussing the law, states it forbids coordinated subscription buying to "save money" by filling patron needs from source libraries.

Basically, such a practice according to the AAP deprives the copyright holder of its rights under the law.

In addition, libraries have been advised by legal counsel that cooperating on cancellations, i.e., targeting a specific title or publisher could lead to charges of restraint of trade and lawsuits under various and sundry laws. We are a careful lot. In response to the rigid approach from AAP and other publishers concerning their "rights" and their revenues, Dick Dougherty former ALA president and on the Faculty at Michigan, among others has called for universities to "take back" their research publication role.

Individual faculty, as a result of the KINKO law suit are facing changes in teaching situations as well. The story, not at all apocryphal is being told and retold on the nets of faculty who have gone back to "their" publisher to get permission to use copies of their own articles in their own classes, only to be informed that the fees would range from $200 to $400.

In response to both these situations, both the prohibition on subscription sharing (ultimately ILL or document delivery of articles) and unreasonable pricing demands for classroom use, the Aqueduct agenda item No. 10 was written.

> Encourage authors to retain the rights to their own written work for their own use, for teaching and for use by their libraries and institutions.

Bill Cohen and I have been going around on this issue for several years.

In a document that develops this idea much more completely, the Triangle Research Libraries working under a two year project funded by the Council on Library Resources to develop strategies and plans for cooperative information resources development in the sciences and engineering, tackles the problem of who owns what, in a straightforward manner.

The practice of assigning copyright to a publisher in exchange for publication, had its first major proponent when Robert Maxwell made the policy an iron-clad rule for Pergamon press in the mid 1950's. At that time is was fairly redundant at least under U.S. law as copyright was created by publication. Since 1976 under U.S. law, copyright exists from the moment of creation (i.e., protection of MSS). So assignment of copyright takes on more meaning in the present system. Copyright is a primary concern as libraries cancel more subscriptions. Document delivery services, such as CARL's UNCOVER, are coming on line, offering 24 hour turn around for faxed articles, with payment of the copyright fee. Although 3 years ago, Elsevier charged $3.50 per article as a copyright fee, for 1993 they are raising the BASE copyright fee to $10.00 and 50 cents a page over 20 pages. So publishers are increasingly seeing copyright fees as a new source of revenue. As Elsevier's profit picture shows, and I recommend you take a look at the *Business Week* article "Global 1000" in the July 13, 1992 issue p. 94 if you think Elsevier is having any problems–this is not because of revenue problems on the publication side.

The funny counter-intuitive part of this is of course, you can't get any article from Elsevier. You have to go to a library collection to get an article. There are three publishers I know of who are running their own Doc. Del. services, and two of them forbid any other Doc. Delivery service to provide copies of their articles. The two "forbid" publishers are Gordon & Breach and Haworth. Williams and Wilkins has also initiated a Doc. Del. service.

In a seminar in which I was the co-chair in September, 1992 for the Society for Scholarly Publishing, publishers (including Elsevier) did admit that they had gone a bit "too far" with "publisher" rights when refusing authors the right to copy their own articles for their own use. But generally they were unsympathetic (as the new Elsevier copyright fee shows) to the question of access to the information they publish for anyone who does not own a local subscription.

But even that isn't enough for some publishers. The TRLN document upset most publishers attending the SSP seminar in Boston. Not because it meant an immediate loss of income to them. In fact copyright fees, as a subsidiary source of income are insignificant at the moment. Other subsidiary rights (such as microfilm) are considerably more important. But in the new world that may be just around the corner, copying-rights will be the new battlefield. You can understand, with that perspective in mind, that even small society publishers felt threatened by the TRLN document. I particularly call your attention to the Advice to Authors section which is an appendix of the document on the last page. A significant change, which publishers are uninterested in providing, is the right for authors to provide, with a notice printed on the first page of the article that noncommercial reproduction is automatically permitted.

Mixing in this brew is the TEXACO case, which was decided by a U.S. District Court (Judge Leval) in July of 1992. According to the document written by the Texaco Trial Team "The Court rejected Texaco's defense and clearly held that making of single copies of articles (including "notes" and "Letters to the Editor" from STM journals registered with CCC (Copyright Clearance Center) is NOT fair use."

The details of the case are so common as to be worthy of mention. A Texaco scientist copied articles, notes and letters from the Academic Press journal *Catalysis* in the Texaco library. The judge said, "Granted, the copiers are scientists, they are using their copies to assist in socially valuable scientific research, and they do not resell the copies. Nonetheless their research is being conducted for commercial gain: its purpose is to create new products and processes for Texaco that will improve its competitiveness and profitability." Chickering testified that he selected articles to copy because they related to the research that he was doing in the course of his employment at Texaco. The purpose of the research was in each case to improve Texaco's commercial performance.

Regarding the interest of scientific authors in securing widespread use and acknowledgement of their work, the judge was harsh.

> It is not surprising that authors favor liberal photocopying; generally such authors have a far greater interest in the wide dissemination of their work than in royalties–all the more so when they have assigned their royalties to the publisher. But the authors have not risked their capital to achieve dissemination. The publishers have. Once an author has assigned her copyright, her approval or disapproval of photocopying is of no further relevance.

The point cannot be made too strongly, I believe, that if authors want to have a say in whether non-commercial research use is to be made of their works, then they cannot routinely, sign over all copyright control to the publisher.

So far I have touched on three major issues in scholarly publication: (1) price, (2) output or size of the literature, and (3) ownership of the literature.

The fourth major issue is the backdrop of technological change, which ultimately can influence all 3 of these issues. Just a note: At the SSP seminar, Ron Rivest, a faculty member in MIT's computer science dept. looked at the assembled librarians and publishers and told them he didn't need any of them for his research. Most of what he gets comes off the NET. He archives what he is interested in himself, and shares research results with others the same way. Needless to say, librarians and publishers alike spent some time after he left assuring themselves that he didn't know what he was talking about.

Rivest may be an exception, but as an exception, he represents a growing minority. Some have suggested the answer to the serials crisis is the networks, yet as Ann Okerson has pointed out, "technology today is creating additional rather than replacement options. It generates additional purchasing requirements. There is very little substitution although substitutability of a very high priced sort is happening in university libraries prosperous enough to load secondary services into their online public catalogs. And unfortunately, there is very little non-proprietary development to facilitate electronic publishing. IN spite of a great deal of rhetoric, largely by librarians and information scientists, about an efficient, university based electronic publishing system, universities are doing almost nothing to create such an academically-based publishing system. For the most part, only a handful of university based scholars are innovating networked publications and projects" Okerson, op. cit. (p. 12).

So "price," while it may be effected by electronics, has so far not effected them. In fact it could be (and is argued by some publishers) that they have had to raise prices because they've had to invest in state of the art fax and computer systems.

OUTPUT. It seems likely, and we need some way to measure it–I'm all ears for an objective measure, that access to computers and databases should increase research productivity–i.e., more output. Any guess.

And finally dissemination. Here is where there is some work going on. The American Mathematical Society is organizing an electronic pre-print service, Elsevier's TULIP project is a gigabyte experiment, and of course you can buy a license that lets you sell articles for ADONIS. But beyond the IEEE/INSPEC and CD-ROM products not much else that could be considered experimental seems to be happening. There are a FEW and I stress few, electronic refereed journals. But even one of them recently went commercial!

Needless to say, this review and the new research reported here, leaves me a bit pessimistic. I think the major new area where academic libraries are going to be looking at what they do and how and why they do it is in the area of decisions on monograph purchasing. Ad Hoc decisions have already been made all over the country. Cut out our German language approval program. Tinker with the University Press purchasing profiles, reduce our social science and humanities intake. And although scarcely spoken, cut radically our science book purchase programs. This last is largely at the behest, nay even the loud demands of many science and engineering departments. Some hard numbers research at LSU suggests this final step is not only inappropriate, it is cost ineffective. Yes, ineffective in terms of cost.

Let me provide some examples that I hope I will have the opportunity to flesh out next year at this conference, for I have not, indeed delivered on my promised topic. The reasons are many, the primary one being that the program we developed last year to cross tabulate purchasing and circulation quite simply doesn't work anymore in our current version of NOTIS. And the files have become so large, that it is now almost impossible to cross circulation data with expenditure data on the main frame. (For those of you who know what I mean, we can't open two files and run them against each other anymore–they are just simply too big.) So we have spent much of the last few weeks (and Sul, Jennifer says you will owe her on this one) figuring out how to get our current cataloging out of just the item records–or circulation record in NOTIS. Believe me, it hasn't been easy since format (bib level M) isn't coded in item records. Turns out that for LSU's records, the simplest way to find the books that we cataloged last year is to run the circulation code (which is different for books and journals) as the "identifier" for monographs. I came up with that yesterday–after struggling with the so called enum/chron field as the "logical" separator–for about a week. And the data is now available, just couldn't analyze it in 12 hours. (Sorry Sul, I had to sleep.)

What I do have is a very brief table that suggests some directions that we will be forced to take as we analyze not only title availability and our unique "program mix" and collecting commitments at our institution, but as we begin to ask are we collecting in a manner that is the most advantageous? This brief chart suggests that in a short time frame, the very inexpensive books we purchased in the BS section–Bible is the subject–were not of immediate importance to our present patrons (see Cirulation Chart). And were actually a less effective use of our funds than the books in Environmental Technology (TD). Although the average cost of the books in Bible was about $24.64 while the average cost in TD was $86.04 or 3 and 1/2 times the cost of Bible books, the utilization rate was 3 times that in religious studies, at least in a very limited time frame. One small piece of the question becomes, do the Bible books have a longer shelf-life or use life that outweighs the initial advantage of the engineering books? At first blush the answer intuition gives would be yes. But even in longer range studies (a three year period), the books in TD consistently get heavier use than do the Bible books. Are we looking at a 10 or 20 year or longer investment term

# Circulation Chart

| BF | PSYCH | | COST | |
|---|---|---|---|---|
| TITLES | 112 | | $3,963.13 | |
| CIRC–1 | 36 | 36 | | |
| CIRC–2 | 20 | 40 | | |
| CIRC–3 | 6 | 18 | | |
| CIRC–4 | 4 | 16 | | |
| CIRC–5 | 2 | 10 | $ PER/CIRC | UTILIZATION RATE |
| TOTAL | 68 | 120 | $33.03 | 0.61 |

| BS | REL | | | |
|---|---|---|---|---|
| TITLES | 201 | | $4,954.15 | |
| CIRC–1 | 32 | 32 | | |
| CIRC–2 | 4 | 8 | $ PER/CIRC | UTILIZATION RATE |
| TOTAL | 36 | 40 | $123.85 | 0.18 |

| LC | EDU | | | |
|---|---|---|---|---|
| TITLES | 60 | | $1,561.81 | |
| CIRC–1 | 26 | 26 | | |
| CIRC–2 | 3 | 6 | | |
| CIRC–3 | 3 | 9 | $ PER/CIRC | UTILIZATION RATE |
| TOTAL | 32 | 41 | $38.09 | 0.53 |

| GN | ANTHRO | | | |
|---|---|---|---|---|
| TITLES | 44 | | $1,692.30 | |
| CIRC–0 | 23 | | | |
| CIRC–1 | 7 | 7 | | |
| CIRC–2 | 6 | 12 | | |
| CIRC–3 | 4 | 12 | | |
| CIRC–4 | 2 | 8 | | |
| CIRC–5 | 2 | 10 | $ PER/CIRC | UTILIZATION RATE |
| TOTAL | 21 | 49 | $34.54 | 0.48 |

| TD | ENV. TECHN. | | $3,612.19 | |
|---|---|---|---|---|
| TITLES | 42 | | | |
| CIRC–1 | 11 | 11 | | |
| CIRC–2 | 5 | 10 | | |
| CIRC–3 | 1 | 3 | | |
| CIRC–4 | 3 | 12 | | |
| CIRC–5 | 2 | 10 | | |
| CIRC–9 | 1 | 9 | $ PER/CIRC | UTILIZATION RATE |
| TOTAL | 23 | 55 | $65.68 | 0.55 |

for Bible? Can we afford that kind of time frame? I've reported elsewhere that the average age of the Mathematics books that our Math faculty uses is about 10 years, i.e., we don't see any use of math books until they've aged quite a bit. Should we be planning on borrowing those books when we need them rather than investing in them now? Are there other institutions whose collections are more intensively used in Bible that we could partner with for our future needs? These are tough questions, especially when young faculty are pushing for tenure, or seasoned faculty are making a case for increased funding for their "special" areas. But they are part of the calculus that we must begin to develop.

In its own way, the serials crisis we are all dealing with is forcing us to begin to use methods for evaluating our purchases that most of us are uncomfortable with. None I would suggest to you, more so than me. I am at heart a traditionalist. But traditional methods cost money and quite frankly the resources don't exist to let us continue to even pretend to business as usual. An ARL director whom I discussed this approach with, suggested I was implying it was time for Kleenex collections. I hope not. But if we are going to continue buying Bible at LSU we need more justification than a faculty member needs it (for whatever reason–future reference, status, to have a "collection," etc.). As hard as we have had to become in evaluating serials, I would suggest, we must become in evaluating book purchasing as well.

# The Role of the Serials Vendor in the Collection Assessment and Evaluation Process

Kathleen Born

## INTRODUCTION

Change is the single dominant factor in the library profession today. It's a struggle to manage change within our institutions. The most immediate change affecting librarians is the change in the level of funding allocated for library resources. Because of the diminished financial resources, library collections are migrating from a primarily print-based collection to accessing information on an as-needed basis. Online environments and computer technology have been instrumental in changing the library organizational structure. With the implementation of automated systems, changes occur in the number of staff needed; the job responsibilities; the work flow; and a closer cooperation has developed between departments as librarians assess and evaluate library collections to ensure the current and future needs of students and scholars are met.

As library budgets become tight, serials collections undergo close scrutiny since a major portion of the library materials budget is spent on the serials collection. Library committees are formed to

---

Kathleen Born is Director, Academic Division, EBSCO's Subscription Services, Birmingham, AL.

[Haworth co-indexing entry note]: "The Role of the Serials Vendor in the Collection Assessment and Evaluation Process." Born, Kathleen. Co-published simultaneously in *Journal of Library Administration* (The Haworth Press, Inc.) Vol. 19, No. 2, 1993, pp. 125-138: and: *Declining Acquisitions Budgets: Allocation, Collection Development and Impact Communication* (ed: Sul H. Lee) The Haworth Press, Inc., 1993, pp. 125-138. Multiple copies of this article/chapter may be purchased from The Haworth Document Delivery Center [1-800-3-HAWORTH; 9:00 a.m. - 5:00 p.m. (EST)].

© 1993 by The Haworth Press, Inc. All rights reserved.

assess and evaluate journal collections. The collection assessment process can be very labor intensive as data is collected to evaluate each subscription. After careful analysis of the evaluation criteria, subscriptions are grouped into categories of (a) core titles–essential to support the curriculum; (b) non-core titles–a secondary tier of non-essential titles and possible candidates for further cancellation; (c) cancellation list–titles which will be canceled immediately. Alternative ways of acquiring access to the title must be considered in the deselection process.

Subscription agents are very actively involved in working with librarians charged with responsibility of implementing a comprehensive review of the serials collection. Today I will discuss three aspects of a subscription agency's involvement with the collection assessment process. First, I will look at the traditional role of the subscription agency in relation to the collection development staff. Second, I will examine the resources a subscription agency offers to the collection development process. Third, I will focus on several issues related to collection management and discuss ways a subscription agency can effectively work with librarians involved in the collection assessment and collection evaluation process.

Until recently, librarians outside of the periodicals department did not think of calling on their subscription agent for information for several reasons:

1. Traditionally, the subscription agency personnel were familiar faces only to the acquisitions and periodical librarians. Nobody in the library knew much about the agency and the services they offered, nor particularly cared.
2. Most librarians did not realize the larger agencies handle all serials, including monographic series, continuations, annuals, irregular series, newspapers, and government documents. It often surprises librarians to discover a major percent of the agency's database is comprised of publications other than periodicals and journals.
3. Perhaps subscription agents had not made an effort to reach out to other library departments whose job responsibilities required information about serials, or the librarian who knew the agent best failed to make their colleagues aware of the re-

sources available from a subscription agency. Over time the relationship between the subscription agency and the librarians within an institution has changed, primarily due to the necessity to exchange information about serials, which absorb the largest percentage of the library materials budget.

One of the most time-consuming factors in an evaluation process is data collection. Time constraints often hamper the librarian's ability to assemble the right kind of data to study the collection. Not many libraries can commit staff to do the kind of in-depth analysis they would like to do; therefore, collection development librarians are engaging serial vendors to compile and assemble data needed to evaluate the serials collection. The serials vendor is the logical source for criteria used in the collection assessment process.

## *SUBSCRIPTION AGENCY'S RESOURCES*

One of the most powerful resources a subscription agency has to assist collection management librarians is the agency's database. Originally, the database of major agencies contained only information necessary to order or service a subscription. Data such as title, publisher, price, frequency, order requirements and claim restrictions were available. As libraries began to automate, the demand for more bibliographic information grew. Agencies began adding the ISSN and classification codes. MARC formats became important, as well as standardizing titles according to AACR2 cataloging rules.

Subscription agencies continued to enrich their database with data to help librarians evaluate collections. Price history, subject categories, language, country of origin, and indexing and abstracting information became part of the title record. Some agencies added whether or not a title is peer reviewed or refereed and if the title is registered with the Copyright Clearance Center. The database of large agencies serves a dual purpose; first, it is a working database to perform the day-in and day-out order processing, invoicing, and servicing of subscription orders. Secondly, it is a significant source of bibliographic data for the library client. For example, a typical record in a vendor's database today would contain not only the title, the publisher name and address, the price, the frequency and publisher ordering and claiming instructions, but also: the ISSN; where the title is indexed; if the title comes with a membership; back issue information; if the price includes the index; when the title's index is published; the subject terms; Library of Congress, Dewey Decimal, UDC and NLM classification codes; the language of the text; the country of origin; and an indication of whether the title is peer reviewed and/or registered with the Copyright Clearance Center.

The databases of large agencies represent undoubtedly one of the richest depositories of serials information in existence anywhere. Building and maintaining this resource is a time consuming, ongoing process, which entails interaction with thousands of publishers. Agencies strive to have their databases reflect the most current information. The information is not only used to process the agencies business transactions, but is used and evaluated by librarians all over the world. In summary, the subscription agency's database has become a source of some the best and most accessible collection management information which can be found anywhere. With this information and the library's subscription orders with the agency, some very useful collection development reports can be created which address concerns and issues surrounding collection management.

## COLLECTION DEVELOPMENT ISSUES

Typically, there are at least six issues to examine before selecting or deselecting a title for your collection. The weight or importance you give each set of factors depends upon the make up of your organization and the exact nature of its information environment. Questions concerning collection development issues revolve around (see Figure 1):

1. Quality
2. Accessibility
3. Manageability
4. Cost and Budget
5. Availability
6. Usage

An agency cannot help you with the sixth issue regarding usage but it can help with the rest. Let's examine these issues and more importantly the collections management reports a serials vendor can construct[1] by compiling the data geared specifically to your library collection.

## *Issues of Quality*

*Titles by Department Report*
*Survey Report by Department*

The quality of the collection is measured by how well it supports the undergraduate needs and the teaching and research of faculty and scholars. Librarians involved in evaluating their collections approach the process by selecting a broad subject field to examine. Recently, the sciences have been an easy place to begin based on the rising costs of serials to support these departments. How well does the collection support the departments? Are there titles in the collection which are no longer relevant or seldom used? How much are you spending? What is the average price per title?

A subscription agency can provide a subject list by Library of Congress classification; however, in many instances, a title may not fit neatly into the LC classification scheme. For example, a title may be interdisciplinary and paid for by one department but used in more than one area of study. If the library has designated each title with a department code or a subject code, a subscription agency can produce a list of titles supporting the programs and research in a particular subject area. The cost of a title and the amount spent on library materials for the department is often a revelation to the deans and faculty members since they seldom realize how much is being spent on their behalf. Sorting the subject list in descending order by price can create some unexpected interest on the part of the faculty members.

During the collection assessment process, collection development librarians seek input from faculty members regarding the importance of the titles to their teaching and research. A survey is

---

1. The reports listed as examples here are available from EBSCO. Other agencies may have similar reports.

## FIGURE 1
### Collection Development Issues and Serials Management Reports

**QUALITY**
How well does the collection support the academic
departments on campus .................................................. Titles by Department Report
                                                                         Survey Report by Department
Who publishes the information .......................................... Report by Publisher
What is the strength of the collection as measured against
   Standard index or abstract ........................................... Index and Abstract Report
   Standard disciplines/subjects ........................................ LC Classification Report
                                                                         Subject Report

**ACCESSIBILITY**
Is it indexed/abstracted? ................................................. Report by Title and Index

**MANAGEABILITY**
How difficult is it to claim a missing issue ............................. Claims Report
How is the title received ................................................ Membership Report
Which titles are licensed with the Copyright Clearance Center ........... Customized CCC Report

**COST AND BUDGET**
Present Cost ................................. Summary Report of Serials Expenses
Cost History/Trends ....................... Historical Price Analysis
Cost by Country of Origin ................ Country of Origin Report
Summary of US Publications Report
Summary of Non-US Publications Report
Future Costs (forecast) .................. Serials Price Projections
Budget Analysis Reports

**AVAILABILITY**
Who else has it? ........................... Current Subscription List
Document Delivery

*131*

often the way to gather faculty input into the evaluation process. Presenting a list of titles and prices by subject gives the basic information; however, the faculty can make more informed decisions if the publisher, the language, and the country of origin, and peer-reviewed information are added to the survey form. A quick and easy survey instrument can be created for faculty input by coupling the data with a Likert scale so that faculty can rank the titles in order of importance, based on a cost/benefit ratio. The results of the survey may be used with other criteria to evaluate the titles.

### *Report by Publisher*

Who publishes the information? The reputation and overall quality of a journal is part of the evaluation process. Sorting your titles by publisher determines if the collection contains material from publishers known for selecting and publishing quality research and information in the field. It also serves as a guideline for determining the relationship between the price and the value of the journal to the library collection.

### *Index and Abstract Report*
### *Library of Congress Classification Report*
### *Subject Report*

During the collection evaluation process, it may be helpful to know how well the collection measures against a list of titles in an index or a standard list of journals in the field. Since subscription agencies can track where a title is indexed, its LC classification code, and assign a subject term, an agency can offer direct assistance in determining the collection strength in a designated field. For example, if your institution is planning an advanced degree in sociology, it would be beneficial to know how many titles which are subscribed to and are also indexed in Sociological Abstracts. By matching the library's titles against the titles in the index, the percentage of holdings and collection strength can be evaluated. The measurement process helps determine if the collection strength is adequate to support the new program, or if titles with minimal usage should be replaced with titles currently not on order.

Measuring the library's titles in a subject area or specific LC classification range against similar groupings in the agency's database provides a broad spectrum for comparative purposes. A subscription agency's database is made up of titles on order for clients worldwide. Such a comparison may reveal titles to include in the collection or to obtain for review.

## *Issues of Accessibility*

### *Report by Title and Index*

When evaluating a collection access, routes to the titles must be ensured. Are all of the titles well indexed? If cancellations are inevitable, it would be beneficial to know which titles are harder to access or which titles are not indexed at all. Index and abstract information can be included on reports with other evaluation criteria or on a separate listing by title.

## *Issues of Manageability*

> *Claims Report*
> *Membership Report*
> *Copyright Clearance Center Report*

The staff time required to manage a title once it is ordered is yet another consideration in the collection evaluation process. If a title is continually delayed or behind in publication or if the library staff spends an inordinate amount of time tracking claims or trying to secure a missing issue, it may be not be worth the effort to maintain the title in the collection. Subscription agencies have several reports to track claims on a monthly, quarterly or annual basis. Reviewing an annual claims report pinpoints problem titles. In addition, librarians have access to publisher dispatch data and check-in information from other libraries through the agency's online services. To help acquire missing issues, subscription agencies have electronic connections to back issue vendors or maintain a database of serials issues for client use.

Membership titles are a management challenge. Which titles are included with the membership fee? A subscription agency can identify the membership title and all of the accompanying titles. This can be done either on an invoice or on a membership report. The membership report makes it easier for the clerical staff to determine the source of an unfamiliar title arriving in the acquisitions area. By consulting the agency's database, you can decide if it is cheaper to purchase the titles separately or as a part of the membership.

Subscription agencies continue to seek sources of information to add value to their database. In an effort to make it easier for librarians to track which publishers are registered with the Copyright Clearance Center, some agencies are incorporating this data into their databases. As a result, you can obtain a list of your subscriptions registered with the CCC, thus saving time and making royalty payments more manageable.

## *Issues of Cost and Budget*

The rising cost of serials is one of the major concerns, if not the primary focus of collection development librarians. The effectiveness of a collection development librarian is often judged by his/her ability to assemble a timely, relevant collection of information at a cost the campus administration has determined to be enough–whether it is or not! Consequently, the issues surrounding present, historical and future costs of serials are of major concern.

## *Present Costs*

### *Summary Report of Serial Expenses*

Subscription agencies are constantly updating their databases with current publisher prices. As many as 175,000 transactions a month are made to EBSCO's title records to ensure the most recent information is available to our clients. Reports listing current expenditures including all billbacks or adjustments are valuable when reconciling the cost of serials with the acquisitions budget. Since reconciliation is an ongoing process, library managers rely on comprehensive cost reports to present the total cost of a title. A summary report of serials expenses produced on a monthly or a quarterly schedule can provide a systematic way of tracking current expenses to ensure the serials budget can support the cost of the collection. If a collection remains fairly stable, the monthly summaries from the previous year provide a point of reference when estimating serials cost for the forthcoming budget cycle.

## Cost History/Trends

### Historical Price Analysis

One of the most frequently requested series of reports offered by a subscription agency are historical price analysis reports. Covering a three-to-five-year time span, the historical price analysis reports supply the collection development staff with a title-by-title analysis of pricing trends by department, by subject, by publisher or by country. These various analysis options enable subject bibliographers, department heads, and collection development librarians to obtain a quick snapshot of changes occurring within the library collection. In addition to the title analysis, summary information at the end of the reports is especially valuable. The statistical data will include the annual and cumulative percentages of increase as well as the average cost to maintain a title in the collection. Cost information specific to the library's collection supplied by an objective third-party source can be persuasive evidence to support the library director's budget request to the campus administration. Additionally, obtaining this information on diskette allows the flexibility of sorting the data by price or percentage of increase. For example, a review can only include titles which have increased 50% over the previous year. If the library is targeting titles over $300.00, sorting options can be rearranged to develop a list quickly. Some librarians are sorting their titles by highest percentage of increase over the time period covered by the report. If you take advantage of the information you can obtain from your agent, you can use it to support your library budget request.

### Cost by Country of Origin

*Country of Origin Report*
*Summary of Non-US Publications Report*
*Summary of US Publications Report*

In the evaluation process it is critical to know the percentage of titles in the collection which originate from non-US publishers and from US publishers. If the collection is weighted with non-US titles, the money spent is susceptible to currency fluctuations in addition to inflation. Price projections are more accurately estimated when one knows the amount spent and the percentage of titles in the collection which originate from non-US or US publishers. Subscription agencies enter the country of origin as part of the title record. Reports can be produced to analyze the number of titles received and the cost of subscriptions by country.

## *Future Costs (Forecast)*

### *Serials Price Projections*
### *Budget Analysis Report*

The budget cycle begins early in the year for most librarians. You are asked to project the amount of money you think you will need to cover the cost of serials price increases for the next fiscal year. Subscription agencies begin receiving calls in January from librarians requesting price projections for the upcoming year. At this point in time, we can both take out our crystal balls and predict a number. Agencies begin announcing preliminary price projections in February and March. Several updated projections are released throughout the year to assist with the budget planning process. At any point during the library's budget planning process, the subscription agent can factor in the price increase projections for non-US and US titles to arrive at an estimated percentage of increase for the upcoming year.

## *Issues of Availability*

### *Current Subscription List*

One of the major considerations in canceling a title is whether another library in the region maintains a subscription to the title. As budget shortfalls continue to plague libraries, cooperative collection development projects become reality. The initial cancellation projects focus on duplicate subscriptions found within the university library system. As state agencies create statewide information networks, such as Ohiolink, to share resources, subscription agencies are asked to provide customized printouts or tapes showing all titles held within an institution or region so duplicate subscriptions can be identified and overlap studies conducted. Libraries will continue to maintain a core list of titles supporting the undergraduate needs and faculty research at the institution. Collection responsibilities for peripheral titles will be shared. The focus is on access rather than ownership of the titles with low usage or titles considered nonessential to the library collection.

## Document Delivery

As libraries move from ownership of information to access to information, a greater portion of the library budget will shift from print journals to electronic access to indexing and abstracting databases and electronic full text of articles. As access methods to information change, subscription agencies will adapt and be around for the long term. If not, they will eventually fold. The present situation is reminiscent of the horse and buggy manufacturers, who went out of business because they thought they were in the carriage business instead of the transportation business. Subscription agencies are in the information business–the business of delivering serials information.

You are witnessing the transformation of subscription agencies from primarily print-based suppliers of information to suppliers of online access to serials information. Subscription agencies will provide a mechanism for librarians to search online files via a current awareness service or table of contents and select articles to purchase from multiple publishers. What does this mean to the collection development librarians? Simply put, your subscription agency will continue to serve as a single source for your serials information needs, either as a single article or as a print journal.

The management reporting mechanisms of these systems will complement the management reports you presently receive. The reports will track the titles which contain the most frequently requested articles. Based on information indicating actual request statistics, collection development librarians can make changes to the collection profile to ensure the library subscribes to the titles it needs.

## *Issues of Usage*

Usage is another factor in the evaluation process. How frequently is the journal used? What is the cost per use? Is it possible to calculate the cost/benefit ratio of access vs. ownership? Librarians implement their own usage studies and weigh the results against other evaluation criteria. Clearly the emphasis is on accessing titles with low usage, particularly if the cost is high.

## *CONCLUSION*

We have reviewed several issues regarding collection management and ways in which the serials vendor can address issues of quality, accessibility, manageability, cost and budget, and availability through cooperative collection building and online access to serials information. Only you know the questions you need to ask in order to study your library collection. Given enough time and enough information, any librarian can assemble the data needed to create the reports for collection analysis. It is a labor intensive process requiring many hours of staff time to compile. An agency can let a computer generate the basic data you need and allow you time to do the intellectual analysis to arrive at a plan for managing your library materials budget and developing strong serials collections.

As a library service supplier, a subscription agency shares a stakeholder relationship with the library. As stakeholders, the library and the agency share common goals. We must continue to work together to exchange information about your serials needs so together we can each deliver excellent service. With mutual communication, cooperation and commitment, we can succeed.

For Product Safety Concerns and Information please contact our EU
representative GPSR@taylorandfrancis.com
Taylor & Francis Verlag GmbH, Kaufingerstraße 24, 80331 München, Germany

www.ingramcontent.com/pod-product-compliance
Lightning Source LLC
Chambersburg PA
CBHW052130300426
44116CB00010B/1846